Mission From Below

Growing a Kingdom Community

— DR JANET HODGSON —

Sacristy
Press

Sacristy Press
PO Box 612, Durham, DH1 9HT

www.sacristy.co.uk

First published in 2018 by Sacristy Press, Durham

Sacristy Limited, registered in England & Wales, number 7565667

British Library Cataloguing-in-Publication Data
A catalogue record for the book is available from the British Library

ISBN: 978-1-910519-77-6

For
Imelda Poole, IBVM (Loreto)

and in memory of
Philippa Green, IBVM (Loreto)

Foreword

Mission From Below is a timely and impassioned reflection on the nature of kingdom mission and spirituality from an outstanding reflective practitioner. Janet broke new ground in the development of local mission in parishes and networks across the Diocese of Durham. The title of this book sums up not just the ministry of presence of two Loreto Sisters in The Clarences, but all of Janet's own ministry as a builder of collaborative missional communities and groups. The Healthy Churches initiative and materials emerged out of Janet's contextual research in the North East. This has largely gone unacknowledged, so I would like to set that record straight.

This current book provides profound insight into Janet's meticulous approach to history and context, characteristic of all her writing. We see this not least in her chapter on the development and character of The Clarences and her setting of Sisters Philippa and Imelda in the historical and spiritual context of Mary Ward and the IBVM. Janet makes reference to Catherine Cookson and the power of story in the culture of the North East. As I read this, I was reminded of the early work of another County Durham novelist, Pat Barker, whose *Liza's England* evokes much of the twentieth-century experience of the people among whom Imelda and Philippa lived and served.

Janet makes it clear from the outset that she has little time for top-down churchy/clerical approaches to mission which are only motivated by getting more people into church. This is by no means, however, a defensive case for doing nothing: quite the reverse, it is a call to vulnerable engagement with alienated and excluded communities who can regain hope and dignity for themselves. As a South African who has had close experience of the struggles against apartheid, Janet naturally draws on the contextual theology of the radical South African Dominican priest, Albert Nolan. The "option for the poor" adopted by the IBVM drinks deeply from the theology of liberation. This is what the sisters lived when they came to Port Clarence. It is interesting, to me at least, that my work in support of Janet was informed by my own reading of Nolan's *Jesus Before Christianity* and *God in South Africa*. Janet had a great grounding in contextual theology before ever she came to the UK.

The beginning and continuing effectiveness of any communication and engagement is listening and paying attention before making any claim on knowing people and their culture. Philippa and Imelda had the courage to make themselves that vulnerable after the pattern of Jesus himself. Out of this listening and quiet loving emerged a quality of servant leadership which rises out of these pages, the kind of collaborative and mutual service which provided the Peace Centre and a prophetic and beautiful approach to ecology in the creation of a garden. Rublev's icon of the Trinity was always an inspiration to the Sisters of real communion being lived in co-operation. These remain profound symbols of regeneration of the self-worth of a community facing devastating disadvantage over generations.

Janet's account of the Sisters' kingdom mission is passionate and admiring, but it is also truthful and unromantic. Jesus' coming to a backwater of the Roman Empire has been called the scandal of particularity. Imelda and Philippa lived this particularity in a distilled way by that Transporter Bridge on Teesside. And they did it in and through Him. Jesus was in Port Clarence ahead of them in the reality of people's spiritual longings and in the belief in God expressed by some of the young men, among others. This book teaches us good lessons about "cross-in- the-pocket" spirituality. I have worked a number of times with Janet and her Images workshops. I commend her insights revealed here about the spirituality of the industrial and post-industrial North East. All that Imelda and Philippa hoped for was rooted in prayer, as all mission must be. Their authentic, holy calling in a post-church environment has much to teach us now and into the future. My continuing thanksgiving for what God did through them will be aided by the prayers they used, which you can find at the end of each chapter.

Mission From Below challenges us to look afresh at our ecology of mission and what components are essential. Janet is not anti-clerical or anti-church. She has several bishops among her admirers, as well as me, like Philip North and Laurie Green. With them, she challenges us here to see the fruits of commitment to the people of poor, outlying estates and the structural injustice under which they live. The story of Imelda and Philippa is a prophetic story about how we fail as the Church if we are not for and with the people among whom they went to live. This book, and Janet's other work, encourage us to be both courageous and vulnerable in our prayer for justice and healing without delay, and in our engagement where that justice and healing are most urgently needed, that Christ's kingdom may come soon.

Stephen Conway
Bishop of Ely

Preface

Why another book on mission? Don't we have enough already? To dispel these scruples something needs to be said in defence of this story about a unique mission right on our doorstep in England. I met the two Loreto Sisters of the Institute of the Blessed Virgin Mary after I was appointed Adviser in Local Mission for the Anglican Diocese of Durham in 1994. Bishop David Jenkins had created this post because he felt that, given the recent closure of the coal mines in the North East of England, and the collapse of industrial alternatives, local mission had become more important than traditional overseas mission in this region. Local mission was precisely what the Loreto Sisters Imelda Poole and Philippa Green, of the Institute of the Blessed Virgin Mary, were doing in The Clarences, a deprived post-industrial estate on the northern bank of the River Tees. They were engaged in a bold experiment in a radical, lay-friendly ministry honouring the local culture and history of these indigent but proud people.

Here, I came face to face with the marginalization experienced by people in the North East. I became aware that their unique and vibrant working-class spirituality had been totally ignored by the institutional Anglican Church. Ambulance ministry tended to be the norm in much of this economically ravaged region. This meant caring for these people's most immediate needs without bothering to analyse and address the reasons for their poverty in any depth.

As background reading for this book I made a particular study of recently published works on mission. Astonishingly, almost all of them voiced a resounding, unequivocal endorsement of "mission from above". There was seldom an attempt to formulate a theology of mission from the people's perspective. Whether it involved the clergy or accredited lay missioners like me, it was all done under the authority of the Church. It was all about mission from the Church, by the Church, through the Church, being imposed on the people of God.

As a lay missioner myself, I was constantly asked why I did not seek ordination and serve the Church as a priest. The assumption seemed to be that in the eyes of God the ministry of lay people did not carry the same worth as that of the ordained. I identified with the Sisters' mission precisely because the thrust of their work was decidedly non-clerical. In public, they kept a low profile as nuns. Although they had been sent by their Order to realize the Catholic Church's concern for "an option for the poor", they had no obvious back-up system. They found work as supply teachers to become self-supporting. As women, they held their own in an otherwise male-dominated clerical context. In this, they followed the example of their beloved Yorkshire foundress, Mary Ward. In the seventeenth century she was way ahead of her time in forming a women's Congregation, which was not enclosed, wore no robes, and was not under the authority of the local bishop.

Christian mission in England, as elsewhere in the world, still seems to be seen as something to be unilaterally designed and implemented by the Church for the benefit of the laity. But the Sisters lived out their conviction that authentic mission in Christ was by the people, of the people, and for the people. This "people-shaped" mission was radical in that it adopted the missionary model of Jesus himself and had the potential to rescue Christianity from the captivity of the institutional Church (see Philippians 2. 1–8; 2 Corinthians 8. 9; Matthew 20. 26–28; Hebrews 2. 17; etc.).

This model holds two key principles together—mission from below and servant leadership. The one cannot exist without the other. Where leadership is exercised with self-effacing humility, we are bound to witness servant leadership as practised by Jesus. This allows the local population to be liberated to think, pray, and act for themselves. Thus empowered, the people, not the hierarchical Church, take the initiative in deciding on the kind of mission that would be best suited to their overall wellbeing. In this book, I have chosen to identify this model as "mission from below". It is contrary to "mission from above", which is dictated by those in power and is normally presented in an all-purpose package without any attempt to listen to the voice of the people or adapt to the local culture, folk religion, and specific history of the region. Whether clergy or laity participate in a mission initiative from below, they would be instrumental in building up a lay-friendly, inclusive Church.

Personally, as a lay woman, I found the idea of working together with two dedicated Loreto Sisters, who had opted to minister in one of the most disadvantaged enclaves in the North East, very refreshing. We became friends and I was soon drawn into their ministry in The Clarences—the name given to the combined estates of High Clarence and Port Clarence. The Sisters were role models in the building up of local women as leaders. In the Church, these women would usually have been relegated to the most menial chores such as cleaning, dusting, polishing brass, and folding leaflets. Now they found themselves playing a pivotal role in the running of community affairs. Equipped with a new self-respect and confidence as part of a large, close-knit family, they were empowered to cultivate their nurturing gifts and do justice to the overwhelming issues that assailed their estate.

The Sisters spent the first two years of their mission as a listening presence in the community. What they heard focused on hassles with benefits, mental and physical illness, bereavement, domestic violence, unemployment, youth crime, alcohol and drug dependency, school truancy, evictions, anti-social behaviour, dealings with unsympathetic civic authorities, waste disposal, and other practical matters which defined the residents' day-to-day lives. Whatever their circumstances or age, the residents were not used to being listened to and this listening ministry established a bond of trust from the start. The Sisters, in turn, found a strong sense of community spirit. No one was ever left to suffer alone. An authentic Christian mission, in which people bear each other's burdens, was already being carried out. In this context, mission was not being formulated in cleverly honed theoretical jargon as in mission workshops and clergy conclaves, but within the concrete framework of a small, socially excluded local estate. The mission strategy was based on real people grappling with real problems. There was nothing academic about this enterprise.

Following this time of listening to people's heartaches and hopes, the Sisters moved on to walking alongside them in support of their struggle for justice and a better deal. The residents felt that they were a forgotten people in a forgotten place, ignored by the authorities. One of their most pressing grievances was fuel poverty. The Council maintained that a pay point for gas and electricity at The Clarences was not economically viable and their nearest pay point was at Stockton-on-Tees. Not only did this involve a costly bus ride, but they were doubly discriminated against because those who could pay by direct debit were charged less. Stirred up by the Sisters, this emotive issue helped galvanize the residents into finally finding their voice. After some lively meetings, which I attended, and a campaign to get a petition signed by the whole community, in which I also played a part, a fuel pay point was finally set up in the Community Centre and was soon paying its way. After this success, the residents were empowered to take action on a host of other issues.

As The Clarences fell on hard times in the post-industrial era, the churches that had been ministering there demolished their buildings and left. When I first visited the estate, there was little Church presence and no church services took place except for occasional Catholic masses in private homes. After the Sisters came, the residents were soon gathering every week to celebrate their solidarity as a community, and their faith in the presence of God in their midst. These gatherings were open to everyone and had a refreshingly non-clerical ambience. No homilies were preached, no creed was intoned, no confession was made nor pardon granted, nor was a collection taken. But the people prayed together, sang hymns, and exchanged the Peace. They felt united by their commitment to making the estate a better place to live in. The Sisters prayed with people when requested, and Bible study groups were formed where opinions were freely expressed, but the Sisters never thrust their faith on others. I consider this a salient feature of their ministry.

Babies were blessed both as a thanksgiving for the gift of life and as a church sacrament. No distinction was made between believers and unbelievers in this cosmopolitan gathering. Generations of Irish Catholic families mingled with the long-standing Roma minority, local northerners, and immigrant newcomers. Young and old, poor and not so poor, those with jobs and a large majority of unemployed, all came together to celebrate life and its infinite possibilities. They were not moved by any dogmatic beliefs but by a robust faith in their shared humanity, which they somehow felt was honoured by God in Jesus. While sharing in the pain of their scarred humanity, they also rejoiced in the hope of a healed future.

The love of the Celtic saints and their spiritual heritage has always been paramount in the folk religion of the North East. The Sisters also revered the female saints of old—Hilda, Brigid, Hildegard, Mechthild, Julian, Teresa—and, of course, Mary Ward, and used their prayers and writings in their personal devotions. This is why a selection has been included at the end of each chapter of the book. Thanks to their ministry, the ethos on the estate became moulded by a blend of the two distinct marks of the medieval Celtic Church's mission—a quest for social equality among people of all ranks and a personal commitment to lead an honest life marked by prayer. The people's prayers reflected a hankering for justice, for an end to their exclusion, for a world free from want and war, for a society where everyone was treated as a child of God. They were without a church but not without spirituality and not, certainly, without a clear sense of their own mission under God.

The goal of the Sisters' mission was never Church growth but Kingdom growth. The Kingdom, however, was not an otherworldly concept in the eyes of the people. It meant a better quality of life here and now, dignity, equity, fellowship, love, trust, sharing, respect, laughter, good health, education, happy children, job satisfaction, a clean environment, celebrating together, and the like. They were totally uninterested in fresh expressions of church, geared towards Church growth, as has been the fashion in contemporary missionary thinking in the institutional Church. Baptisms at ecumenical services, with each minister baptizing according to the respective family tradition, were conducted in two phases on successive Sundays: firstly, catechism of the particular denomination, and, then, the baptism itself which truly epitomized the cohesion of church rite, family tradition, and local culture. This allowed everybody to bond with God in the best spirit of North East ecumenism.

The celebration of secular events became the norm, involving anything from family visits, a leave-taking, an anniversary, a recovery from illness, or a major achievement. All that was conducive to peace, healing, and harmony provided a ready excuse. As in the ancient Celtic Church, the Sisters' mission was about celebrating the extraordinary in the ordinary, and seeking the spiritual in the most mundane happenings of everyday life.

Another matter of immense missionary significance was the promotion of prayer and meditation. The Sisters set apart a Peace Centre where people could go just to be quiet, especially after a death or in times of difficulty. They were encouraged to sit still before God and communicate with him directly without any sort of mediation. There was a growing appreciation of the power of silent invocation of God's solace and healing into one's life. Pilgrimages to an ancient church high up on neighbouring hills were also organized. Candles were lit in petition and in memory of the departed. Even the children would regularly knock on the Sisters' door asking for a prayer before going happily on their way. The formal theology and liturgy of the institutional Church are miles away from the local customs and the folk spirituality of the North East. In their home-run Bible studies, the residents' groups learned to do their own rustic theology and rediscover their own spirituality.

The Sisters initiated an eco-friendly project in surrounding their Peace Centre with a garden, and this legacy has now taken wings. Landfill sites adjacent to The Clarences had become a dumping ground for both hazardous and non-hazardous waste, including radioactive material. Protests and petitions achieved nothing. But with the help of a retired Chief Superintendent of Cleveland Police working alongside them, the very worst piece of land was cleared of lorry-loads of asbestos and fly-tipped waste to create a flourishing community garden. Caring for the earth has now become a central plank of the residents' mission from below. Men and women, young and old, the mentally challenged and the disabled, veteran soldiers and ex-criminals, members of neighbouring churches, all have come together on this regeneration project. Excess produce is left on the doorsteps of the needy. The garden continues to expand and will include training facilities for young people. This will equip them to be self-employed, the dearth of jobs being another major issue.

Imelda and Philippa finally left The Clarences in 2004 after sixteen years of singular service. This was much longer than they had anticipated, but it allowed them to build their unique ministry on strong foundations and so their legacy lives on.

I have been watching the movement of the Holy Spirit stirring in this deprived estate in the North East for more than two decades. From being betrayed by both Church and State, and being designated the worst place to live in England, it has grown into a community with a soul, a faith, and a mission to pray and work for the Kingdom. Thanks to the servant leadership of a number of people, including the headteacher of the primary school, a retired senior police officer, the editor of the community newspaper, and numerous local women and their action group, this once forgotten place is now poised to write a new chapter in the mission from below. I hope that the institutional Church may allow itself to be evangelized by this missionary model of a Kingdom community on the River Tees.

In conclusion, I can do no better than recall the benedictory words addressed by Peter to another forgotten community two thousand years ago:

> But you are a chosen race, a kingdom of priests, a holy nation, a people to be a personal possession to sing the praises of God who called you out of the darkness into his wonderful light. Once you were a non-people but now you are the People of God; once you were outside his pity; now you have received pity.
>
> *1 Peter 2. 9–10*

Acknowledgements

I am deeply indebted to Imelda Poole IBVM (Loreto) for her many contributions to the book. They include her notes, photographs, and a number of unpublished reports to her Congregation about the two Loreto Sisters' work at The Clarences. I am particularly grateful to her for her generosity in sharing the prayers that the Loreto sisters used in their daily worship. As followers of Mary Ward, their work was based on prayer and meditation as well as active involvement alongside the residents of the estate. A selection of contemplative prayers or reflections has been placed at the end of every chapter. In addition, Imelda has continued to support me in the publication of this book and in helping it to reach a wider audience.

In 2015, I paid a return visit to The Clarences. Jean Orridge OBE, headteacher at the High Clarence Primary School, was able to bring me up to date with what had taken place on the estate after the Sisters left. A small group of her pupils gave us a guided tour of this amazing school. By chance, the Clarences Residents' Action Group (CRAG) was meeting at the Hub that day and allowed us to sit in on its discussions. Thanks to Jean, we had a further meeting with members of the group over tea at the school.

We were also fortunate that Pat Chambers, editor of the *Billingham Community Newspaper*, was present to make arrangements for the annual Christmas party and she has provided me with further information. Kevin Pitt was our other lucky find that day. As a retired Chief Superintendent of Cleveland Police, he has worked alongside the residents of The Clarences to create a huge community garden on former wasteland. We were given a personal tour of the garden and were delighted to see all that has been accomplished and to learn of all the future plans (see Chapter 12).

Thank you to the Stockton Archives, The Revd Robert Cooper, Sr Imelda Poole, Kevin Pitt, and Julie Hodgson for allowing use of their photographs. My daughter, Carol Yarnold, is to be thanked for her proofreading of the manuscript, and for providing me with her delicious food and many acts of kindness and support. These have included regular shopping expeditions and her gardening expertise. In coming to terms with failing eyesight from age-related macular degeneration (AMD) and related difficulties, I am grateful to my family—Mike and Julie, James and Arlene, Alastair and Tracy, and my grandson, Miles—for their help in many different ways.

I have also been blessed by the kindness and thoughtfulness of friends, relations, and neighbours, without whom I would have struggled to keep going—Dr William Rowland, Dr Ann Haw, Linda Godlonton, Professor Christine Schnitzler, Phyllis Palmer, Lyle Jobling, and Barbara Manson with her kundalini yoga. They have seen me through good times and bad, and have always been there for me.

A special word of thanks goes to the Revd Jayant (Jay) S. Kothare for his unfailing support and encouragement over nearly thirty years in the production of a number of books. Even though he lives in Manchester, England, his editorial advice and theological input have added greatly to the substance and direction this story has taken. He accompanied me on my visit to The Clarences in 2015, which allowed him to have a first-hand experience of the many issues involved in presenting this case study. We were delighted to see all the good things that are still happening in this courageous community.

Bishop Stephen Conway, Bishop of Ely and former Archdeacon of Durham, has done me a great favour in writing the Foreword to the book at short notice. During my seven years as Adviser in Local Mission in Durham Diocese, he chaired my three-person support group and was a tower of strength in encouraging me to explore new ways of doing mission. I am forever grateful for his kindness, guidance, and support.

Lastly, I wish to thank Richard Hilton and his team at Sacristy Press in Durham for all they have done in the preparation and publication of this book. It has been an honour to work with them, particularly as I am now resident in South Africa and grappling with visual impairment. I thank them for their patience and perseverance.

Contents

Nuns Hit "Ghost Town"

In 1986, the headlines in local newspapers in North East England were dramatic in heralding the arrival of two Roman Catholic nuns in The Clarences. This is the collective name for Port and High Clarence. The "ghost town", as it was called, is on the banks of the River Tees, north of the Cleveland Hills and North York Moors.

Nuns hit ghost town

Nuns will blaze trail on estate

Nuns to help run-down area[1]

The nuns were Imelda Poole and Philippa Green. Known as Loreto Sisters, they belonged to an international apostolic order of women, the Institute of the Blessed Virgin Mary, founded by Mary Ward, a Yorkshire woman, in 1609.[2] The Clarences, to which the two Roman Catholic Sisters had come, was described as "grim with boarded up homes, tumbledown shops and the gloomy all-over greyness of a 'ghost town'".

The estate had some of the highest levels of unemployment in the country, up to 85 per cent. Much of this was long-term, spanning a few generations, and to work is to live. Widespread poverty, chronic ill health, and a pervading sense of hopelessness had been exacerbated by low standards of education, few unskilled work opportunities, a poor diet, inadequate living conditions, a dearth of basic facilities, and overwhelming industrial pollution. But it was precisely because the estate was regarded as one of the most deprived in England that the IBVM Congregation had sent the Sisters there to begin a pioneering grassroots ministry.

Since the late 1960s, the Roman Catholic Church in Britain had encouraged some religious orders to embark on community development through a ministry of presence and active service. Fr Austin Smith, a Passionist priest, was a pioneer of this type of inner-city mission. He lived and ministered in Toxteth, Liverpool, for nearly forty years. An outspoken advocate for disadvantaged communities, he dedicated his life to working with the poor and the powerless in their struggle to survive, and to combating racism and discrimination in all its forms.[3] He was to give the Sisters much invaluable advice as they faced their new challenge.

The Clarences, however, were not always so economically and socially deprived. This made their present state of post-industrial dereliction even more tragic. In their heyday, more than a century earlier, they had helped bring in the Industrial Revolution. Port Clarence, originally known as Samphire Batts, had been established when colliery owners in County Durham had needed better access to the North Sea to export their coal. Ships had become larger and could no longer navigate the shallow waters up river to the original port at Stockton-on-Tees.

The Clarence Railway, opened in 1833, connected Stockton to new termini at Haverton Hill and Port Clarence, lower down on the north banks of the Tees. They had deeper water at low tide and could accommodate the colliers shipping coal to cities like London. They both had their own railway stations when local roads were still being built. Later that century, the main channel of the Tees was dredged to deepen the river for shipping, and a harbour was built in the estuary to extend coal and other exports. Miles of reclamation banks lined the sides of the river, an economical way of acquiring new land. The Tees now bustled with shipping activity day and night and Port Clarence, serving new industries, was busier than ever.[4]

Figure 1: The Port Clarence Railway Line (left),
1910 (Stockton Library Service, T394)

The Clarence Railway was named in honour of the Duke of Clarence, later King William IV. Horses were used for the first two years before being replaced by steam locomotives. However, the railway had a major rival, the Stockton and Darlington Railway (S&DR) to Middlesbrough. In the 1820s, a group of Quaker businessmen had bought the Middlesbrough farmstead and estate, and had set about establishing a new coal port on the south bank of the Tees. The S&DR, which had opened in 1825, became the first public railway in the world to operate a freight and passenger service. When this lucrative trade was extended to Middlesbrough in 1830, the expansion of the port was ensured. The town, which had been founded to provide labour, became an industrial hub.[5] The Clarence Railway shared the S&DR rail track to the Durham coalfields, but their restrictions and ruinous charges prevented it from becoming profitable, so it was eventually taken over by others.[6]

The Clarences have a history of Irish immigration, starting in the late 1800s and continuing to around 1920. The Clarence Railway Company was recruiting labour to work the coal wagons and man the staithes, the waterside coal depots equipped for loading vessels. Others worked as seamen. The Irish immigrants came particularly from the counties of Tyrone, Monaghan, and Wicklow, in Northern Ireland, after the potato famine. They were also employed in the burgeoning iron, steel, and chemical industries and, after the First World War, the Furness shipyards. The population of Port Clarence rose from 22 in 1851 to 853 twenty years later, more than half being Irish. This gave rise to a strong Roman Catholic community with Irish roots. The rest were mainly from the North East.[7]

In 1854, Isaac Lowthian Bell, a metallurgist and industrial chemist, and his two brothers began recruiting a workforce for their Wylam Iron Works based at Port Clarence. This was helped by the discovery of iron ore in the Cleveland Hills. The iron works soon replaced the railway as the main employer of a steady supply of Irish labour. Isaac Bell was described as a formidable giant of a man, but rather abrasive. He received many honours in engineering and amassed a fortune in the process. He was twice Lord Mayor of Newcastle-upon-Tyne, a Liberal Party Member of Parliament for North Durham, and was made a baronet.[8]

Figure 2: The Bell Brothers Iron Works at Port Clarence, around 1920 (Stockton Library Service, T4046)

The Bell brothers began pig iron production with three blast furnaces at their Clarence Iron Works. The largest in Britain at the time, the firm had an annual output of 200,000 tons by 1878. The works had an ideal river frontage and a large acreage of land for the disposal of slag. According to Ann Appleton of Port Clarence, whose history of this period has provided a mine of information, tons of slag were used to make firmer foundations on which to develop the iron works.[9]

Bell and a partner were the first in the world to manufacture steel rope and submarine cable. The Clarence Iron Works produced iron for bridges and steel rails for railways across the British Empire. The Bell Brothers company also operated its own ironstone mine and limestone quarries in Weardale, the hill country to the west cresting the River Wear. They employed about 6,000 men in mining and manufacturing, who laboured long hours, living and working in grim conditions for abysmally low wages. By 1920, iron and steel dominated Teesside.[10]

As Port Clarence grew, the Bells built dwellings for their workers in close proximity to their blast furnaces. These one-up-one-down houses were erected back to back in rows of terraces. The village's growth attracted the services of a grocer, a butcher, an inn and, by 1871, a policeman. In 1874, the Anderson Foundry Company, which manufactured every kind of railway equipment, was established to the west of the ferry landing. However, most of its workforce came across the river by steam ferry from Middlesbrough.

By the turn of the century, Port Clarence boasted a post office, a Roman Catholic school, and a reading room cum library. In 1859, the new Anglican Church district of St John the Evangelist was formed and a large church was built in nearby Haverton Hill in 1865 to serve the area. The Roman Catholic school initially functioned as a church for the Irish community on Sundays. Since the time of James I at the beginning of the seventeenth century, there had been very few Catholic families in the surrounding area, although Port Clarence is said to have been designated a parish since 1865. The coming of the Irish immigrants was a significant boost to their numbers, leading to the building of St Thomas of Canterbury Church. It opened in 1900 with seating for around a thousand people.

The mother and grandmother of Mary Whitaker (née Appleton) were born in the "Old Port", as it was known, but her maternal grandfather came from County Tyrone in the early 1900s to work in the iron foundries. She remembers that, even during the 1950s and 1960s, St Patrick's Day was always celebrated with a school concert and the wearing of shamrocks sent by relatives in Ireland.[11]

In 1907, Florence Bell, the second wife of Isaac Bell and a writer and playwright, published her seminal account *At the Works: A Study of a*

Manufacturing Town (Middlesbrough). Florence's impressions of Port Clarence are surprisingly penetrating:

> Many of the dwellers in the place have as deeply rooted an attachment to it, as though it were a beautiful village. There are people living in these hard-looking, shabby, ugly streets who have been there for many years and more than one who has left it has opined to be back again . . . for many of the dwellers in these cottages, as those who have frequented them, have a veritable keen zest in existence, a fund of human sympathy, and a spirit of enterprise as applied to mental as well as physical toil.[12]

Some better housing included "Gaffers' Row" for the foremen and bosses working for the Bell brothers. This extended the village beyond the iron works, and allotment gardens provided a more varied diet. Ann Appleton relates that, even though the workers were exposed to the rigours of industrial life, the village remained small and so retained the character of a rural community characterized by close relationships. Florence Bell's description has many parallels with what the Loreto Sisters experienced nearly 80 years later. The sense of belonging and community spirit had remained strong despite dire living conditions and deprivation.

Salt had been panned in nearby Greatham and Seal Sands since Roman times, over a thousand years previously, and the salt industry had continued during the medieval period. Large fires were lit to evaporate the sea water and crystallize the salt, leaving huge mounds of ash behind. Over time, these were grassed over. In 1874, John Bell drilled north of the river and discovered a vast exploitable salt bed at Saltholme Farm, near Haverton Hill, and a salt works was established there. Using improved techniques, liquid brine was pumped up and then heated from hot slag to produce dry salt. This was used to make soda and for other chemical and industrial purposes.[13]

Figure 3: Brine Pumping Wells, Port Clarence
(Stockton Public Library, T14097)

After a few years, the Bell brothers sold their boreholes to the Salt Union. In 1894, the formation of the Greatham Salt and Brine Company gave local industry a boost. Finally, these works were taken over by the salt-making company Cerebos, of Bisto gravy powder fame. The salt industry became one of the main employers, easy access to the river providing ready export facilities. The surrounding villages expanded accordingly. A good number of labourers in the salt works at Haverton Hill came from Cheshire after the salt mine at Winsford was closed.

During the First World War, neighbouring Billingham set up a plant to produce synthetic ammonia for use in explosives. In 1920, Brunner Mond took over the works to make agricultural fertilizer.[14] It then merged with another company to form Imperial Chemical Industries (ICI). In 1932, the plant employed around five thousand people and continued expanding as new industries were added. In the 1960s, atmospheric pollution from a boiler and sulphuric acid plant was such that all the buildings in Haverton Hill had to be demolished. Most people moved to Billingham. The ICI plant was later demolished and replaced by a light industrial estate.[15]

During the First World War, the Furness Shipyard was established at Haverton Hill to replace ships sunk by German U-boats. After the Second World War, larger ships and tankers were built. When the shipyard changed hands, it expanded to produce steelwork for structures such as bridges. Despite modernization, the yard was closed in 1968 with the loss of 3,000 jobs. It was eventually nationalized in 1977 and placed on a "care and maintenance order". Much of the structure remains rusting away, a relic of the past.[16]

The most arresting landmark in the area, seen from miles around, is the Middlesbrough or Tees Transporter Bridge. Opened in 1911, it replaced the steam ferry service connecting Middlesbrough on the south bank of the river with Port Clarence on the northern side. After much discussion, Parliament had finally ruled that only a transporter bridge could be built so as not to interfere with the river traffic. Its overall length is 851 feet (259 m), leaving a span between the two towers of 590 feet (180 m). The clearance above the river is 160 feet (49 m). During the Second World War, the bridge was hit by a bomb but remained in working order.

Figure 4: The Tees Transporter Bridge (Imelda Poole)

The longest surviving transporter bridge in the world, it has a travelling car or gondola suspended beneath it. The gondola can carry 200 pedestrians, nine cars, or six cars and one minibus, across the river in 90 seconds. The locals refer to it as "the Transporter" or, more fondly, "The Tranny".[17] In 1985, its historic importance was recognized when it became a Grade II listed building. Since then, floodlights and a visitors' centre have been added. It has provided the setting for a good number of films and television programmes. One BBC series caused much alarm among the locals when it portrayed the dismantling of the bridge and its re-erection in North America. A disclaimer had to be issued after the final episode to say that the Transporter had remained untouched.[18]

Mary Whitaker recalls that, by the mid-twentieth century, many houses had two rooms with a small kitchen downstairs and two or three bedrooms upstairs. Back yards were surrounded by high brick walls with a door opening out onto the back street. The toilet was also in the yard and there would be a small garden out front. She remembers that there were quite a lot of shops in Port Clarence in those days. A small parade at the end of Queen's Terrace comprised a newsagent cum sweet shop, a butcher, and two grocers. A fish and chippy stood near St Thomas' Church with a Co-op and a post office shop.[19]

High Clarence also had a fish and chip shop and post office.[20] Situated beyond the school, it was regarded as a different place from Port Clarence. Before it was demolished, Haverton Hill was different yet again. It had plenty of shops, including a chemist, doctor's surgery, barber, baker, butcher, and several food shops. Altogether, it was a fairly self-contained community. Middlesbrough was seen as their town rather than Billingham or Stockton. Using the Transporter Bridge, Billingham was within walking distance and the trip only cost a penny. As a child, Mary attended St Thomas' School, as did most of her friends. In those days, it also had a senior school, but she went on to St Joseph's Convent in Hartlepool, the girls' Catholic Grammar School, and then to university.

Mary had many happy memories of her childhood in Port Clarence. She would spend long days playing in the fields and the "stell", making dens and fishing for tiddlers and newts, or in her father's allotment. The swings near the Cenotaph, later a car park, were another attraction. Her first Saturday job was in a local shop, Frank Vernon's. As a teenager, dances on Saturday evenings were in Haverton—the "Haverton Hop"—or in the "new" community centre in High Clarence. No drinking was allowed. That came later when the Railway Club opened in Middlesbrough. Then there would be a rush to catch the last Transporter ride at midnight.

Prayer of Thomas Merton (1915–1968)

My Lord God, I have no idea where I am going.

I do not see the road ahead of me.

I cannot know for certain where it will end.

Nor do I really know myself,

and the fact that I think that I am following your will

does not mean that I am actually doing so.

But I believe that the desire to please

    You does in fact please You.

And I hope I have that desire in all that I am doing.

I hope that I will never do anything apart from that desire.

And I know that if I do this You will lead me by the right road

though I may know nothing about it.

Therefore will I trust You always though I may seem to be lost

and in the shadow of death.

I will not fear, for You are with me,

and You will never leave me to face my perils alone.

Thoughts in Solitude[21]

CHAPTER 2
"The Valley of the Dry Bones"

The imagery of the Valley of the Dry Bones is taken from Ezekiel 37. 1–14. In the sixth century BC, Ezekiel is faced with the task of repairing the fortunes of Israel in one of its darkest hours. God grants him a vision in which he finds himself standing in the middle of an arid valley littered with dry bones. The valley is a metaphor for Israel, an exiled nation in Babylonian captivity, which had ossified socially, politically, culturally, and spiritually. It had become bankrupt both materially and in terms of faith in God. God asked the prophet to convey the assurance that He would breathe life into the dry bones and restore them with sinews and flesh. Israel would be resurrected into a people with a new faith and a new purpose. The awesome prophecy comes true and the scattered dry bones come alive with new life.

At the end of the twentieth century, the North East of England could be visualized as a Valley of Dry Bones. The dereliction was so vast that the only way hope and life were going to return was through the grace of God, which would renew, heal, and restore the people to a life of self-respect and purpose. This applied not only to the North East in general, but also to The Clarences in particular.

This northern region, once the powerhouse of the British Empire as regards heavy industry, coal mining, and shipbuilding, had been dealt a death blow with the demise of these industries and was now in terminal decline. Life had never been easy for the working-class labourers, even in earlier times. Over the years, they had taken action with strikes and hunger marches to draw attention to their plight—their miserly wages, dangerous working conditions from a young age, unsavoury terraced housing with poor sanitation and cramped quarters, ill health, and high mortality rates. But the response to any organized protest was invariably punitive, the supposed ringleaders being imprisoned or laid off and their families forcibly evicted from their homes. Power was in the hands of the wealthy few, whether they were leading industrialists, coal-mining barons including the aristocracy (like the unpopular Marquess of Londonderry), eminent politicians, or even the Church of England hierarchy. Class defined the establishment and those with the right connections could rely on government support in suppressing any resistance. The workers were powerless and at their mercy.

The writer Catherine Cookson (1906–1998) was born in Tyne Dock, near the mouth of the River Tyne in East Jarrow. Her prolific output of historical novels and autobiographies provides a graphic account of the poverty-stricken life of the working-class environment in which she was reared. As depicted in *Our Kate* (1969), the heavy industrial dockland was dominated by wooden jetties, railway lines, workshops, and warehouses. She was the illegitimate daughter of an unmarried barmaid. After leaving school at thirteen, she first worked as a servant and then in a laundry. Her Geordie humour cannot disguise the hardships she suffered in these squalid surroundings: the violence and abuse, the looming fear of the workhouse, the trips to the pub to fetch drink for her alcoholic mother. She escaped by moving south to manage a laundry in Hastings. After her marriage to a grammar school master, she triumphed to become Britain's most widely read author with sales worldwide worth millions of pounds.[22]

In 1852, Jarrow's former coal industry had been followed by the founding of Palmers Shipyard and Iron Company Ltd. More than a thousand ships were launched there in the next eighty years. But mismanagement and changing world trade conditions led to the closure of the shipyard in 1934, a devastating blow. When a proposal to replace it with a modern steelworks plant was opposed by the British Iron and Steel Federation, an employers' organization with other plans, the workers had no recourse but to take action against their widespread unemployment and impoverishment.

In October 1936, the Jarrow Hunger March or Jarrow Crusade, as proclaimed by their banners, was the most significant protest of them all. Before leaving Tyneside, around two hundred selected men were blessed by the Suffragan Bishop of Jarrow at a church service. Afterwards, he was forced by the Bishop of Durham to apologize publicly for this apparent misdemeanour. Led by their doughty Labour MP, Ellen Wilkinson, the men marched to London, taking twenty-six days. They carried a petition requesting Parliament to re-establish industry in their town. Along the way they were supported by all the political parties. The march achieved little in socio-economic terms. The House of Commons did not even bother to debate their petition. But it gave witness to the tremendous courage and endurance of the people against historic circumstances over which they had no control, and the power of the establishment. In her book, *The Town That Was Murdered*, Wilkinson, a socialist, feminist, and trade union organizer, gives an angry indictment against the injustice of the system, which had brought so much misery to her constituents.[23]

Following the termination of the shipbuilding, iron, and steel industries, and the forced closure of the coal mines, the decline and deprivation of the North East continued unabated in a downward spiral. In his Cuthbert Lecture in 2000, the Very Revd Geoff Miller, Archdeacon of Newcastle, presented some damning statistics to show how the disappearance of traditional industries had a haemorrhaging effect on the region's economy and social structures. This included a higher proportion of people claiming income support than in any UK region except Northern Ireland. Poor educational attainments meant that men no longer had economically useful skills. Those in the workforce were less qualified and received lower wages than almost anywhere else in the country. The region also contained some notorious housing and community blackspots, but the people stubbornly refused the help that was offered to them. They were likely to be passive if not truculent.[24]

Local churches, thanks to their inward-looking mindset, indulged in a romanticizing of the past together with a defiant resistance to change. Battling under siege, they failed to face up to present realities and manage decline. In the 1990s, the OXLIP index of deprivation listed 67 benefices in the Anglican Diocese of Durham as Urban Priority Areas. As one churchwarden in a working-class parish told me: "We are permanently geared into survival and maintenance. Our energy is consumed with preserving our tradition. We feel powerless and should close the church but it is like pulling out the life-support of a 'vegetable' patient with the grief involved." In The Clarences, they had taken the plunge and over the years had demolished all five churches belonging to the different denominations.

Figure 5: The Old School, Port Clarence, where Irish Roman Catholics first worshipped, 1983 (Stockton Public Library, T7216)

Industrial dereliction, urban decay, unemployment over a number of generations, never-ending poverty, homelessness, chronic ill health, premature mortality, violence, and substance abuse have been the all-too-visible signs of the breakdown of a once integrated and hard-working society, and the social stress that this has involved. Poverty, embracing every facet of life, is experienced as powerlessness and resignation to a future without hope. Family networks remain significant, but they can form closed entities within the wider whole and exclusive groups within a church, creating divisive factions. Infighting is a habitual mode of response, tearing the church and community apart. The men were accustomed to hardship and danger, but being unemployed was an agonizing blow to their self-worth and status as the main breadwinners.

Girls used to leave school at a young age and either enter domestic service or work in factories. Women are now taking up poorly paid, part-time employment as cleaners or in supermarkets without any long-term security or benefits. But it is the young people who are worst affected. Without any future prospect of work, they see no point in acquiring an education and take refuge in vandalism, petty theft, criminality, and escalating drug and alcohol abuse. The lack of any sense of purpose in life among young people is dehumanizing. In Port Clarence, the bad reputation of the estate lingers on as an added disadvantage. One 21-year-old man, signed to a work agency, put it this way: "If you come from here people think you are worth nowt. Every time I get past the first stage for a job, I say I am from Port Clarence and it stops there. They think the worst."[25]

When I took up work as the local mission adviser in Durham Diocese in 1994, a former pit village might sport a memorial to men lost in a mining disaster, or some of the mine's old headgear still stood tall, but otherwise all traces of the colliery would have been landscaped and grassed over as a nature reserve or else transformed into a housing estate. The pit's proud past, once the lifeblood of the community, would have been obliterated as if it had never existed except in memories and old photographs. Similarly, all that is left of the county's once-thriving industrial sites are the rusting relics of abandoned plants and derelict wasteland. The shipyards remain silent and deserted too, their idle cranes and gantries a ghostly reminder of their past glory.

The Clarences contained around 350 households, with about a thousand residents.[26] As an urban remnant, they were isolated by miles of empty space. In the vicinity, the still-functioning ICI chemical works, the largest of their kind in Europe, spewed forth toxic fumes day and night. This industry relied on contract work rather than jobs for life, and required expertise with computers and technical equipment that was beyond most of the locals' reach. The low standard of education has remained problematic. In the High Clarence Primary School, very few parents have benefited from higher education. About three quarters of the pupils are eligible for free school meals, well above the national average. A large proportion of them are also designated as having special educational needs, whether these comprise learning difficulties or social, emotional, or behavioural problems.[27] A high level of mobility does not help. Few children have any pre-school experience and the teachers work wonders in getting them up to standard.

The terraced housing was mainly rented accommodation, but there were some low-cost privately-owned dwellings. Many of these buildings were boarded up and just left to rot by absentee landlords. Regular flooding caused by blocked drainage canals made for unpleasant living conditions. In 2013, the Tees broke its banks and some three hundred homes and businesses had to be evacuated, adding to the estate's woes.[28]

When the Sisters came, nearly one third of the homes were headed by a single parent. Local amenities were pathetically inadequate, with minimal health provision, no chemist, a couple of badly stocked and infrequently opened shops, three dilapidated pubs, no sporting facilities, and sparsely situated public telephones. Fly-tipping and arson were perennial problems. I personally saw stolen cars burning in the fields and the wreckage of others lying abandoned. As recently as 2012, a wood recycling plant was set alight by arsonists and burnt for nine days. Some young men were taken into custody, but no one was charged.[29]

Debt was the most pressing issue, however, weighing heavily on the residents as the cost of living continued to spiral. Most families lived permanently on the dole, while the elderly tried to survive on miserable pensions. Loan sharks thrived, charging extortionate rates.

Such was the poor quality of life on the estate that in the late 1980s it was threatened with closure and the removal of the entire population, as had happened at Haverton Hill. What with unreliable transport facilities and the abysmal provision of public services, The Clarences felt totally abandoned and forgotten, justifying the title of "ghost town". As a local newspaper reported: "Many of the families have been here for generations. They've watched the life slowly ooze out of the place, the jobs in the foundries and on the railway line long gone, neighbours moved out, the once friendly terraces crumbling."[30]

**Figure 6: Watching the Gondola of the
Transporter Bridge (Robert Cooper)**

The historic Transporter bridge was unreliable, often closed due to bad weather or repairs. When it was actually functioning, shops in central Middlesbrough on the opposite bank of the Tees were beyond the Clarence community's means. Car ownership was low and, with the irregular bus service, shopping trips to the nearest towns of Stockton-on-Tees and Billingham were a luxury. But although The Clarences might exemplify the problems of "social exclusion", the residents themselves had a strong sense of identity and belonging, with a defiant pride in their past, and refused to disappear. Few moved away. As a local Labour councillor explained: "Their grandparents' names are on the war memorial, and as far as they are concerned this is their home."[31] Apart from anything else, the majority did not have the wherewithal to uproot and start again elsewhere.

The war memorial or cenotaph is a central feature of The Clarences and the former Haverton Hill. Erected after the Great War, the memorial records the names of local men who lost their lives between 1914 and 1918. Headstones in the St John the Evangelist graveyard in Haverton are almost all that are left of this old Anglican church and provide other names. A good number of men, some very young, signed up for service in the West Yorkshire Regiment battalions. In such a small community, there cannot have been many people who did not lose a relative or close friend in the war. Their descendants have gone to great lengths to trace their particulars, the internet proving to be an invaluable asset in the process. The exchange of memories makes for fascinating reading as former friends, neighbours, and family members renew contact and fill in the gaps.

In times past, the war memorial was a favourite meeting place for local men on a summer's evening. After a hard day's work, they would sit on a bench nearby and relax with a smoke while chatting to their neighbours.[32] Remembrance Day services at the war memorial have always been well attended, starting with a procession through the estate led by neighbouring church choirs, town councillors, and the veterans. In 2014, the centenary of the outbreak of war was marked by a special service.

Despite the injustices visited upon this community, all was not doom and gloom. The Loreto Sisters were to find much that was positive. There was the friendliness, loyalty, resilience, neighbourliness, generosity, good humour, and an enduring community spirit. There was also a fervent regional identity, an undying pride in the past, and a deep-seated reverence for their Celtic heritage with its great Northumbrian saints.

The coming of the Sisters to the estate was treasure beyond belief, steeped as they were in the spirituality of the Yorkshire founder of their congregation, Mary Ward. Her concern for justice for the poor and the disadvantaged, based on a life of prayer, was exactly what Imelda Poole and Philippa Green hoped to bring to The Clarences.

The Celtic Heritage of Northumbrian Saints

The Homily of St Hilda of Whitby (c.614–680)

Trade with the gifts God has given you.
Bend your minds to holy learning that you
may escape the fretting moth of littleness
of mind that would wear out your souls.
Brace your wills to action that they may
not be the spoil of weak desires.
Train your hearts and lips to song which
gives courage to the soul.
Being buffeted by trials, learn to laugh.
Being reproved, give thanks.
Having failed, determine to succeed.[33]

Prayer of the Venerable Bede (673–735)

O Christ, our morning star,
Splendour of Light Eternal,
shining with the glory of the rainbow,
come and waken us
from the greyness of our apathy,
and renew in us your gift of hope.[34]

Bede on St Cuthbert (c.634–687)

He was before all things fired with divine love, sober-minded and
patient, diligent and urgent in devotion and prayer, and friendly
to all who came to him for comfort. He held that to give the weak
brethren help and advice was a fit substitute for prayer . . . When
he had the opportunity he also laid hold on the way of life of a
hermit, and delighted to stay in solitude for no short space of time

and to be silent and apart from the conversation of mankind for the sake of the sweetness of meditating on God.[35]

CHAPTER 3

The Vision of Mary Ward (1585–1645)

Mary Ward was born in Mulwith, near Ripon, North Yorkshire, in 1585, of staunch Catholic stock.[36] At the time, Catholics were being persecuted in England, but she still spent much of her childhood with Catholic relatives and her spirituality matured in their devout households. As a small girl, she lived with her grandparents on a remote estate, chosen so that she should not give away family secrets. On occasion, they had been forced into hiding and her grandmother, whom she described as "righteous, Catholic in belief and unshakeable in her adherence to it", had been imprisoned.[37]

Soon after Mary returned home in 1595 their house was burnt down during anti-Catholic riots and they had to move again. As a beautiful young woman, she had many suitors from Catholic landed families. Neville, a scion of the Earl of Northumberland, was one, but by then she had become certain of her religious vocation. At that time women had little choice but to get married or follow a cloistered life in a convent.

When Mary turned sixteen, she was required by law to register as an Anglican. For safety's sake, she was sent to Catholic friends, where she followed a strict religious regime. Despite family pressure to marry Neville, she prayed for strength to remain faithful to what she believed was a calling from God. Her father had been imprisoned in London and, after his release, she joined him there. Her Jesuit confessor also favoured her prestigious marriage, but a sign while saying Mass convinced him of her sincerity.

When Mary came of age in 1606, she entered a monastery of Poor Clares at Saint-Omer in northern France, then part of the Spanish

Netherlands, as a lay sister. The following year she founded a monastery of the order for English women at nearby Gravelines. By 1609 she was due to be professed in the Poor Clare convent as an enclosed monastic nun. Just before the event, she was led by God to believe that this was not for her, much to her confessor's displeasure. Unsure of her new direction, she returned to England to await further illumination through constant prayer. As she said: "My suffering was great, but bearable, for He who imposed it, bore the burden too."[38] Meanwhile, she cared for those in need, working in prisons and private homes while spreading her faith in secret.

Figure 7: Mary Ward

Throughout this time Mary had been spiritually directed by the Jesuits and was inspired by their way of life. In 1609, she had thoughts of joining the Carmelites. Later that year, however, she experienced what she called her "Glory Vision". She believed that what God was asking of her would give Him great glory. By then, other women had joined her and were waiting to be guided on their way forward. Finally, in 1611, Mary had another vision which directed her to found a religious congregation. Modelled on the Jesuit constitution and way of life, and with the Father General's permission to follow the Society's rule, she added her own original conception of an order exclusive and peculiar to women.

What emerged was an apostolic congregation of women called to serve God in whatever way they could in responding to the greatest needs around them. Traditionally, the work of female religious was confined to prayer and ministry that could be done within the walls of a monastery.[39] Mary envisaged that female religious would live in companionship while engaging in an active ministry in society at large. They would not be constrained by a cloistered existence, or wear religious habits. They would also be free from an established rule under the governance of the local bishop. She sought self-government under direct papal jurisdiction.

The move from enclosure to an open, fully apostolic life for women was unheard of at the time and the new institute suffered much at the hands of the Church. But Mary soon attracted a devoted band of followers working under her guidance. Once established as a religious community at Saint-Omer, they opened a school for girls where they were taught reading, writing, sewing, and the principles of Christian life. Mary believed that women were equal to men in intellect and should be educated accordingly. "There is no such difference," she said, "between men and women that women may not do great things . . . I hope in God it will be seen that women in time to come will do much."[40]

The empowerment of women through education became a central feature of their work, but as the institute developed they branched out to serve wherever they saw a need. Mary's enduring passion to liberate women, and her missionary zeal to seek justice for the poor, were centuries ahead of her time and have largely been ignored historically. As she told her companions: "Cherish God's vocation in you. Let it be constant, efficacious and loving . . . Be seekers of truth and doers of justice . . . Be kind and merciful towards the poor and do not call them beggars . . . That we be such as we appear and appear such as we are."

The setting up of new communities and schools expanded as Mary travelled over much of Europe, mainly on foot. This included several crossings of the Alps in winter. With a few companions, she walked the 1,500 miles from Flanders to Rome to present her plans personally to the Pope, and appeared several times before the cardinals to plead her cause. Some members of her institute were sent under cover to England to support the work of priests. Above all she was a woman of prayer. Her writings show her "deep relationship with God whom she served in confidence and trust".[41] In her *Autobiography* and Resolutions in 1619 she related that:

From an early age I have loved the virtue of integrity and therefore
it is unnatural or rather impossible for me to act half-heartedly
in anything pertaining to the things of God. The soul is invited
to give all and the response should be an entire surrender of self.
I venture to declare that in my experience I see that the above
dispositions are gifts from God to any person he chooses, but
particularly to us women who seek to walk the way of the spirit
. . . Divine love is like a fire which cannot let itself be shut up,
for it is impossible to love God and not want to work to extend
God's honour . . . My deepest longing in everything I do is that
God be content.[42]

The community flourished but was controversial, attracting censure and
strong opposition from within the Church. At the time Europe was torn
by religious dissension and women's rights were unthinkable. English
Catholics were divided too, while the Jesuits were subjected to widespread
suspicion and hostility. Mary Ward's use of their practices as a foundation
for her own spiritual development added to the animosity against her.
Her congregation was derided as the "Jesuitesses" and she was prevented
from founding a religious institution according to her vision. This led to
its suppression in 1630.

In a letter from prison the following year she wrote: "It is good pleasing
the Friend of friends and labouring in eternal work, and above all to be
entirely and forever at our Master's disposal."[43] Again, in 1633, she wrote:
"What does it matter what becomes of me so long as I do what my master
sent me here for?" Fortunately, Empress Catherine the Great of Russia
supported her educational innovations for women and she moved there
for a time with most of her companions. This enabled her vision to revive
and develop further.

At the invitation of Pope Urban VIII she then went to Rome, where
she gathered together younger members under the protection of the Holy
See. Pope Urban later described her as "a woman of great prudence and
of extraordinary courage and powers of mind, but what is much more
. . . a holy and great servant of God". With his support, she returned to
England with her companions. Starting off in London, they established
free schools for the poor, nursed the sick, and visited prisoners. In 1642,

she finally moved north with a few followers and established a convent at Heworth, near York. She died there three years later.

Her companions feared that her grave would be desecrated in the city, so she was buried in the Osbaldwick churchyard about a mile away from York. According to the record, "the [Anglican] vicar was honest enough to be bribed."[44] She was admired and revered by many local people, both Catholic and Protestant, and Anglicans were among those who attended her burial. Her legacy spread throughout Europe, her followers being known as "the English ladies". Of worldwide significance is the fact that she provided the model for most modern women's congregations.

After the institute's suppression, it was not allowed to acknowledge Mary Ward as its founder. At last, in 1707, Pope Clement XI granted the rule official papal approbation, declaring that women should be governed by women. In 1745, Pope Benedict XIV approved the Constitution of the institute, and the founding of the original institute was confirmed by Pope Pius IX in 1877. But Mary Ward was only publicly acknowledged as the Foundress of the Institute of the Blessed Virgin Mary by Pope Pius X in 1909. In 1982, Pope John Paul II named her with the great saints of northern Britain as "that extraordinary woman from Yorkshire". Finally, in December 2009, she was declared Venerable by Pope Benedict XVI. She was recognized as "a woman of heroic virtue". This was the first step on the way to being canonized as a saint.[45]

Members of the IBVM are commonly known as the Loreto Sisters, their name being taken from the shrine at Loreto in Marche, Italy, where Mary Ward used to pray.[46] Historically, there were three main branches—Roman, Irish, and North American. In 2003, the last two combined to form the Loreto Branch. The Roman Branch was permitted to change its name to Congregatio Jesu or The Congregation of Jesus. This was regarded as being closer to Mary Ward's vision of a Jesuit order for women.[47]

The order's remit is to work "to integrate our active apostolic spirituality in community for mission with the conviction that our mission is to stand in a direct way with the powerless, those on the fringes of society".[48] Today, the Loreto Sisters are engaged in a wide variety of ministries in twenty-two countries on five continents. They have a particular concern for the marginalization of women. From the order's inception, the education of girls has been a priority, although some schools are co-educational. So far, they have set up 170 schools worldwide, educating over 70,000 pupils. Their other work has included community outreach programmes, assisting disadvantaged women and children, managing shelters for homeless women, care for the aged, literacy programmes, spiritual direction, counselling, aboriginal welfare in Australia, and human trafficking in vulnerable communities in Europe.

In the 1980s, the order committed itself to "a preferential option for the poor".[49] Consequently, Imelda and Philippa were directed to find a suitable place where they could live out this missionary calling. Discernment is central to Mary Ward's spirituality, and this involved a lengthy process as the Sisters sought to discover God's will as to where they should be sent. Three grassroots communities were considered—two in England and one in Wales. After studying detailed reports on each place, they decided on The Clarences. The Sisters felt called to this particular community as it seemed to be so completely divorced from the rest of society and by far the worst off.

Mary Ward's Prayer

O Parent of parents, and Friend of all friends, without entreaty you took me into your care and by degrees led me from all else that at length I might see and settle my love in You.

What had I ever done to please You? Or what was there in me wherewith to serve You? Much less could I ever deserve to be chosen by You. O happy begun freedom, the beginning of all my good, and more worth to me than the whole world besides.

Had I never hindered Your will and working in me, what degrees of grace should I now have. Yet where as yet am I?

My Jesus, forgive me, remembering what You have done for me and whither You have brought me, and for this excess of goodness and love let me no more hinder Your will in me.

Autobiography, 1619[50]

CHAPTER 4

A Listening Presence

Despite the deprivation in The Clarences, Imelda and Philippa were surprised to find a close-knit, caring community which welcomed them with open arms. The immediate difficulty was that the Sisters were not eligible for a council house. Fortunately, the authorities supported their wish to be a church presence on the estate. The Residents' Association then chose a small three-bedroom terrace house with a little garden front and back. When the Sisters arrived, they found their new home boarded up and still under repair to make it habitable. It had been damaged by fire and an attempted break-in. Although this was not the most auspicious start, neighbours rallied round to help and they had soon settled in. This was the beginning of lasting friendships.

The Loreto Sisters brought with them a wealth of experience in education that was to be invaluable. Philippa had been headteacher in two Catholic primary schools, and in a Loreto middle school in North Wales. Then, after studying psychology and psychoanalysis, she moved more specifically into child guidance. She worked for ten years as an educational psychologist in Moss Side, Manchester. Finally, she became leader of the Mulwith Community in Islington, London, and then a Retreat Director at Loyola Hall, Liverpool.

Imelda had taught in three secondary schools, and was chaplain in two of them. After studying counselling part-time at Manchester University, she worked as a youth employment training officer, and was co-founder of the Youth Foundation, Kings Corner Project, for deprived young people in London. This was followed by part-time work and training in the ministry of spirituality at Loyola Hall and in Dublin. She then took up a part-time post in this field at the Catholic Ushaw Seminary in the North East, as well as being responsible for formation ministry with temporary professed Sisters of the English Province of the IBVM (Loreto) congregation.

Once they came to The Clarences, they had no problem in obtaining work as supply teachers in local schools, such as in Hartlepool. In order to achieve their goals, they needed to be self-supporting and pay their bills. Imelda also worked one day a week for a few years as the Family Liaison Teacher for the High Clarence Primary School. In addition, they were widely used for spiritual direction and counselling, as well as playing an active part in various women's groups outside the estate.

Despite their wide experience, Philippa and Imelda found the two years spent in selecting the site for their new mission a huge learning curve. They had both become increasingly frustrated with the inadequacies of the statutory services in understanding and meeting the real needs of people on the margins of society. Even so, they were to find it an immense challenge to shake off the negative reputation of The Clarences and to restore hope in what seemed to many people to be a hopeless situation. For a start, they had difficulty in forming a clear understanding of the specific mission to which they had been called. How were they to interpret Jesus' command to go out into this new world? As Imelda later reflected:

> We arrived knowing only that we believed deeply in the Gospel of presence and befriending and that through the ministry of listening to the people in this place whatever the creed, colour or race, we would be led from day to day to know how we were called to be and how we would respond to the greatest needs, alongside the other residents.[51]

Fr Austin Smith had told them that the physical reality of being with those who are suffering gives credibility to utterance, as the poor and the marginalized do not have the energy to bring about change alone. But living alongside them gives a prophetic base to express solidarity, and this can lead to liberation for all concerned. As Imelda understood it, "this liberation is a freedom from all that holds status and exclusivity as important and which upholds the gospel values of humility and inclusiveness as the path to new life".[52] After much prayer and consideration as to how they might live out the criteria for their new ministry, the Sisters identified six aims:

1. To live a simple, poor life among the people.
2. To be available to respond to the greatest needs of the area where possible.
3. To be involved in the work of building Christian community in the area.
4. To work with other faith communities if they existed in the area.
5. To evangelize and be evangelized by living in the area.
6. To be conscious that initially their mission would be for a limited period of time before being evaluated and assessed.

Mobility was a cornerstone of their congregation's constitution, yet they knew that empowering others can sometimes take a long time.

For the Sisters, mission was "an uncertain way of life in which one is constantly listening to God, present already in the world; and being open and sensitive to the manner in which He was leading us to co-operate in His mission alive and active in other people" (cf. John 13).[53] Within this loose strategic framework they felt called to a ministry of listening and presence, but had no idea where this would lead them. They would leave that to the Holy Spirit. Their goals would remain flexible and there were to be no imperatives or restrictions. People were not going to be managed and would be free to come and go as they pleased. In fact, the Sisters were soon involved on so many different fronts that they stayed for sixteen years.[54]

For the Sisters, one of the attractions of the place was the absence of any church. The Anglican parish church of St John the Evangelist, in Haverton Hill, had been pulled down in the late 1960s and only the lych-gate and graveyard remained. In Port Clarence, the Wesleyan Methodist church, built in 1902, had been demolished in 1970. Both the temporary Anglican iron chapel and the Primitive Wesleyan Methodist chapel had also long gone. St Thomas' Roman Catholic Church, built in 1900, had been the last to be demolished, in 1978. This left the Sisters unfettered by denominational structures or dominating clerical leadership.

In the North East, the laity often have a "father knows best" attitude towards their clergy, while many clergy still follow a hierarchical model of leadership. This can lead to unhealthy power relations, with the laity being relegated to a subservient role. They are not encouraged to live out their faith in any active way, such as challenging the structures that perpetuate their oppression. Good works abound, but are usually limited to ambulance ministry, to bringing succour to those in need in their neighbourhood.

From the start, Imelda and Philippa found that mission was already happening in The Clarences, that "the spirit of God, the spirit of love, was still very much alive".[55] The highs and lows of life were shared by the community as a whole. There was always someone ready to help those in trouble, no matter what the difficulty might be. No one was ever left to suffer alone. The Sisters also experienced the spirit of God moving in their own lives, enabling them to come alongside those who were suffering with mutual respect and a loving heart. They were supported by their belief that Jesus was interested in the story of every single individual. Each one needed to be listened to in order that God's love might be seen and heard in the midst of their troubles, as well as in their goodness, laughter, and joy.

**Figure 8: Terraced Housing at The Clarences,
1935 (Stockton Public Library, ST4-46)**

Listening is a powerful tool in reaching people where they are. It is about allowing them to talk, to tell their stories, and to be heard. In evangelism, it is about acknowledging a person as an active participant in the process, rather than being treated as a passive object on the receiving end. True listening entails compassion, empathy, and solidarity. It creates genuine relationships and equitable encounters. God whom Jesus invoked and prayed to was a listening God. This God listened to the cry of the suffering Hebrew slaves: "I have heard the cry of my people." (Exodus 3. 7). This is how he introduced himself to Moses. Because God listened, still listens, and will continue to listen with mercy and compassion, we have a mandate to listen before engaging in any sort of transformative action.

Listening also entails careful observation. Not only are the poor and disadvantaged not heard by those who could change their lives, but they are also largely ignored as if they were invisible. In Luke 7. 44, the unnamed woman waits on Jesus, anointing his feet with perfume and tears. The apostles rudely ignore her, taking her to be just another intrusive female. Jesus gently chides them by asking, "Have you taken notice of her?" Listening and looking are two vital ingredients in any personal interaction.

For the Sisters, remaining faithful to this calling meant responding in trust to wherever they were led. It also meant being open to radical change in a community that was getting such a raw deal. Alienated from the rest of society, the residents felt that they were a forgotten people in a forgotten place. They resented being controlled by faceless bureaucrats and never being listened to by those in authority. A succession of community development workers had seldom stayed for long, regularly being moved on to other work, which was said to have a higher priority.

The Sisters were committed to a befriending and healing ministry, which embraced all aspects of mission. Their aim was to come alongside people to assist them in every possible way without ever taking control. Theirs is a classic example of how a community can be empowered to assume responsibility for its own welfare and development. Women, in particular, were enabled to achieve goals that were quite beyond their wildest dreams, being inspired by the Sisters' own example. The beauty of this relationship was that both the Sisters and the women experienced transformation in their personal lives. As Imelda explained:

> You know that film where the teacher asks the pupils to get up and stand on their desks. He asked them to do that to help them see things from a different perspective. It's been like that for me, seeing life from a different perspective—the way people here see and experience life. We're often cushioned in life from the darkness of what life is like for those who have nothing or very little. Once you see things from a totally different perspective, that perspective colours everything. It changes you.[56]

The first two years of the Sisters' ministry were spent in looking, listening, watching, and waiting. This was a true ministry of presence. Not only did they visit every house on the estate, but they listened to people on the streets and in various groups, such as the local community liaison group, mothers with toddlers, the many single parents, bored teenagers, and the pensioners' group. The community in turn kept open house, with children bustling around. Wherever the Sisters went there was always time for a welcoming cup of tea and a chat, stressing the need for flexibility.

In addition to hearing about the practical difficulties in people's daily lives, the Sisters took a particular interest in their spirituality. Even after three generations of being without any church, a majority still regarded themselves as "believers" and tried to follow the principles of their faith. They had fond memories of attending Sunday school and regular worship. Some would have gone to church up to three times on a Sunday, no matter their denomination. Many still had a profound belief in God and prayed every day, while some still read their Bibles. Imelda made notes of her conversations so that she and Philippa could reflect and pray about what they had heard. Her unpublished report on "Spirituality in The Clarences" provides a unique record.

One woman expressed the need for forgiveness and for the chance to say how sorry she was for anything she had done wrong. In a similar vein, another had a great fear of dying and of what death would bring her. She worried that she might go to hell because of her "misspent" life. They were comforted when told of God's great love for them and reminded of their own loving care of their families over the years. An older man doubted whether many really had an active faith: "Most people live for the day. You live and you die. Money is the real issue that takes up most of the thinking time. Maybe some believe in something after life but they keep this private." A good number who had lost close friends, family members, or children had failed to come to terms with their bereavement and were still struggling to cope with their grief. One woman who had experienced much loss in her life carried some of her father's ashes around in a locket.

There was a widely held belief in reincarnation because, as one woman argued: "If this didn't happen what would be the point of life?" The only wish of another was that when she was reincarnated she would not be as poor as she had been in this life. For her it had all been too hard. A destitute younger woman said she was confident of going to heaven when she died because she had already experienced so much hell here on earth.

Imelda saw the need for a quiet place on the estate where people could find peace in times of trouble and feel close to God. Pilgrimages were organized to the ancient church of St Peter at Osmotherley, on the slopes of the Cleveland Hills in North Yorkshire. Standing above the ruins of Mount Grace Priory, an old Carthusian monastery, the pilgrims savoured the deep spirituality and quietness of the place. Many candles were lit for loved ones who had passed away, and for friends and family who were facing difficult issues. The healing of memories was a priority, and a memorial service held by the Sisters at Port Clarence was well attended.

A surprising number of young men talked freely about their faith in God. They felt that he was a real presence in their lives, even though their prayers might be limited to crisis situations. In contrast, girls in their late teens seemed to have no sense of God or of any sort of spirituality. The general feeling was that life was for living day by day: "You take it as you find it, make the most of it, and that is that." If somebody rubbed you up the wrong way, you shrugged your shoulders and walked on. There was nothing other than this. But even if they had no thought for the future, all were scared of dying. They dreaded any pain, and were concerned that their families would find it difficult to cope with their loss. Imelda was worried about their inability to reflect more deeply on life. Her one hope was that communal worship might provide a starting point.

What surfaced repeatedly in the listening process was the intense isolation felt by the community. As their survival became ever more challenging, the systems designed to help them became increasingly impersonal and constricting. The social services were seen as remote, bureaucratic, and demanding. The desire to be heard and an overwhelming feeling of powerlessness were recurring themes. The cruel manifestations of poverty were another constant, as was the plight of the young people. They were caught up in a circular treadmill of despair. They had to submit to various forms of training, then after failing to find work they returned to the dole.

For one and all, the joy of being really listened to by the Sisters was something few had ever experienced. It gave them space to tell their stories, share their problems, and express their beliefs. A report by the NESF (National Economic and Social Forum) on the Loreto Sisters' work summarized their ministry perfectly:

> They do not have a specific project but see their role as listening to the people about their concerns and helping them take action to address certain issues. They self-reference not as social entrepreneurs but more as workers for social justice helping the local people themselves to take action and find solutions.[57]

For Imelda and Philippa, their own spiritual life was enriched by prayer and meditation. They had a little room set aside as their private, holy place with a crucifix, candles, cushions, and religious imagery. Reflection on the Gospels helped them to remain open to where the Holy Spirit was leading them. They visited the prison, hospital, and hospice too, while home visiting opened the way for counselling and rapid response work. The crises could involve the physical abuse of women and children, family feuds, homelessness, a lack of furniture and the basic necessities of life, bureaucratic issues, illness, and death. They were called out at all times of the day and night. Clear boundaries had to be established as to the limits of their involvement, such as not being used to taxi people around, except in an emergency.

Meditation

Let thy soul walk softly in thee,
as a saint in heaven unshod,
for to be alone with silence
is to be alone with God.[58]

Contemplative Prayers of Mechthild of Magdeburg (c.1207–c.1282/94)

A medieval mystic, Mechthild of Magdeburg is thought to have been born in a noble Saxon family and claimed to have had her first vision of the Holy Spirit aged twelve. In 1230, she became a Beguine in Magdeburg, and later a Dominican tertiary. Her prayers are lyrical musings.

I Cannot Dance

I cannot dance, Lord, unless You lead me.
If You want me to leap with abandon,
You must intone the song.
Then I shall leap into love,
from love into knowledge,
from knowledge into enjoyment,
and from enjoyment beyond all human sensations.
There I want to remain, yet want also to circle higher still.

God Speaks to the Soul

And God said to the soul:
I desired you before the world began.
I desire you now
as you desire me.
And where the desires of two come together
there love is perfected.

Those Who Love Much

Those who love much,
they are silent and truly blessed.
Those who love little,
they preach much
and betray the mystery.

From **The Flowing Light of the Godhead**

CHAPTER 5

Cross-in-my-Pocket Spirituality

As they became ever more deeply entrenched within community life, Philippa and Imelda were inspired by the courage of the people and their ability to keep going despite seemingly impossible conditions. The Sisters found that just sitting with people without being impelled into action was a humbling experience. As regards evangelization, the residents responded openly and thankfully to prayer. On a practical level, the nuns' presence was inextricably linked with an expectation of their pastoral care. This involved help with everyday needs like clothing, cooking facilities, and bedding, without which many people would have struggled to survive in winter. The locals were also generous in helping one another and the sharing of food took on a sacramental quality.

In the absence of regular sacramental ministrations, the locals had drawn strength from the innate spirituality of popular religion. This was particularly evident at funerals, when the community dealt with grief through home-grown rituals. There was the imaginative use of their own heartfelt oratory, the singing of well-known hymns, simple prayers, and silence. This went together with symbols drawn from the context in which the deceased person had lived, like a child's favourite teddy bear, uniting the mourners in a way that formal liturgies could never have achieved.

In my mission work in the North East, I discovered a spirituality that was deeply rooted in the regional culture, irrespective of whether there was a Church presence or not. Over the centuries, the people themselves had incarnated their faith within their daily experience in order to make sense of their lives. Their ancient Celtic roots, folk beliefs, traditional customs, and Geordie savvy had all played their part, as had their social, political, and economic circumstances. In The Clarences, a strong Irish Roman Catholic tradition had been passed down through many generations, enriching their spiritual heritage still further.

In my own workshops around the region I used images of Christ from all over the world to help people think creatively about their faith, unfettered by doctrine or dogma. I collected a sizeable portfolio of pictures showing Jesus in diverse moods, representations, and acts as narrated in the Gospels. This proved to be an invaluable tool in allowing even the most reticent participants to unlock and express their innermost thoughts, feelings, and beliefs in an uncritical and supportive environment. During group work, participants were invited to select an image of Christ which spoke to them on a personal level in relation to a series of questions—Who is Christ for me? Who is Christ for my church or community? Who am I in Christ? How do I live out my faith in Christ? In telling their stories, people felt free to express their doubts as well as their certainties. The overwhelming popularity of a few selected images provided a penetrating insight into the corporate spirituality of the North East.[59]

"Christ the Good Shepherd" was a favourite, as were the "Gentle Jesus" paintings by Margaret Tarrant (1888–1959), with Christ surrounded by small animals and children. Indeed, all images of Christ with children were popular. People who had suffered so much unrelenting hardship in their lives were drawn to a loving Christ who wrapped his arms around them and protected them in times of trouble. As the shepherd who looks after his flock, or a parent watching over his children, he would care for their needs, comfort them in times of sorrow, heal their wounds, and lead them gently on when things got tough. What they were looking for was security and safety in a menacing world. A warm, accepting, and protective image of a loving Lord and Saviour was what they wanted.

**Figure 9: "Suffer the Little Children"—banner at the
Miners' Gala, Durham, 2015 (Robert Cooper)**

Although the Durham coalfields have long been closed, the former mining communities still treasure their banners. Every Lodge of the more than one hundred pits had a distinctive banner, a symbol of their identity and belonging. As one old miner told me: "Our banner was at the heart of our pit." Most sported political or socialist imagery, but a good number had religious themes, perhaps influenced by the Primitive Methodism of chapel folk who earlier dominated the mines. The banner with "Suffer the Little Children" was photographed at the annual Miners' Gala in Durham. The pit folk continue to come together from all over the county for their annual Big Meeting. After listening to some rousing socialist speeches, they then parade through the city. Walking proudly behind their banners and brass bands, they make their way to Durham Cathedral for a closing service. Other religious imagery on banners included "The Good Samaritan", "The Widow's Mite", "Jesus Calming the Storm", "The Good Shepherd", and biblical texts.

Another popular image in workshops was "The Light of the World" by Holman Hunt (1827–1910). Here, the evangelistic message of Christ patiently knocking on the door of our hearts invites us to repent and let him in. The overgrown garden and the brambles obstructing his way symbolize all that makes for personal sin, selfish greed, and worldliness. But it is the glowing lamp held by Christ that is contextualized in popular religion: "It's like a miner's lamp, see." It was a symbol of hope: that Christ as the light of the world would overcome the darkness in people's lives and lead them safely through their many difficulties, just as the miners' lamps had led them to safety deep down in the pits. A reproduction of this painting is a much-loved possession in many homes, passed down over generations as a family heirloom. Local people also identified with pictures of a suffering Jesus in real-life situations. These images spoke of his being with them in their own suffering. They were on the cross together.

The close attachment to religious medals and laminated prayer cards is another sign that a loving God is an integral part of popular religion. In The Clarences, the cards, readily available in markets, are exchanged in times of trouble, illness, and bereavement. They offer consolation that God is with them at all times and that in the end all will be well. They are also thought to be infused with spiritual power, providing tangible protection. Much treasured, they can be found pinned onto a kitchen notice board or a handy cupboard door. Favourite poems and images include "Footprints", "If", Albrecht Dürer's *Praying Hands*, "The Sand Dollar Legend", and "The Gate of the Year", as it is popularly known. The last, by Minnie Louise Haskins (1875–1957), was published in 1912. Originally called "God Knows", it was popularized by the royal family and inspires great comfort to the bereaved:

> I said to the man who stood at the gate of the year, "Give me a light that I may tread safely into the unknown." And he replied,"Go out into the darkness and put your hand into the hand of God. That shall be to you better than light and safer than a known way!" So I went forth, and finding the hand of God, trod gladly into the light. And he led me towards the hills and the breaking of day in the lone East.[60]

The prayer cards were described by one man as "Pick-me-up Prayers". He laid his hands across his heart as he said, "I read one and I feel smashing".

Another much-loved poem by Henry Scott Holland, "Death is nothing at all", is found in most homes and provides much solace:

> I have only slipped away into the next room ... Whatever we were to each other, that we are still ... Life means all that it ever meant. It is the same as it ever was; there is unbroken continuity ... Why should I be out of mind because I am out of sight? I am but waiting for you, for an interval, somewhere very near, just around the corner. All is well.[61]

Figure 10: Cross-in-my-Pocket (Julie Hodgson)

However, the "Cross-in-my-Pocket" prayer, tucked into a little hand-sewn plastic canvas sachet and embossed with an embroidered cross, is the most popular of all. Some also contain a little embroidered cross.[62] They come in various colours, but black or purple yarn is used as a sign of mourning. They are kept in a pocket or handbag as a religious relic that can be felt, fingered, or kissed as a constant reminder of God's protective presence. In popular religion, there is no need for the mediation of an officiating clergyman. As with a wooden holding cross, just carrying or holding the cross-in-my-pocket sachet becomes a prayer in itself.[63] The words say all that is needed. The author of the poem below, Vera Mae Thomas (1901–?) was American, but nothing else is known about her.[64]

I carry a cross in my pocket,
a simple reminder to me
of the fact that I am a Christian,
no matter where I may be.

This little cross is not magic,
nor is it a good luck charm.
It isn't meant to protect me
from every physical harm.

It's not for identification
for all the world to see.
It's simply an understanding,
between my Saviour and me.

When I put my hand in my pocket
to bring out a coin or a key,
the cross is there to remind me
of the price He paid for me.

It reminds me, too, to be thankful
for my blessings, day by day,
and to strive to serve him better
in all that I do or say.

It's also a daily reminder
of the peace and comfort I share
with all who know my Master
and give themselves to His care.

So, I carry a cross in my pocket,
reminding no one but me,
that Jesus Christ is the Lord of my life,
if only I'll let him be.

The process of translating the gospel into contemporary cultural forms has been going on since the start of the Christian era. The Incarnation itself was an act of translation, the Word of God translated into the flesh of Christ within a particular social reality. This process was then extended through the contextualizing of Christ's teaching in four quite different Gospels. Subsequently, the "infinite translatability" of Christianity meant that, as it expanded across the world, it was able to transform and be transformed by the receiving cultures. Moreover, it was the people themselves, not the Church, who took the initiative in drawing on indigenous thought patterns, imagery, symbolism, and myth to establish vernacular expressions of their new-found faith and to relate it to their everyday experience.[65]

As has happened over the centuries, this translation process will take new forms as Christianity continues to interact with local cultures in quite different contexts. In Britain, this might be within inner city conurbations, housing estates, industrial developments, rural settings, or regional areas. *Inculturation* is the term commonly used to describe the symbolic exchange that takes place in the ongoing dialogue between the form in which the Christian faith is presented and the receiving culture. Over time this will be incarnated as an indigenous expression of Christianity.

The inherent spirituality of popular religion, with its rich storehouse of imagery and symbols, cannot be separated from formal Christian beliefs and practices. It is deeply ingrained within the life and soul of ordinary people, nourishing them spiritually and giving their lives added meaning. The challenge is to value its creative aspects and provide opportunities for people to grow in a lasting faith that is grounded in the love of Christ.

There was no doubt that God was ever present in The Clarences, if not in the shape of the Church. Popular religion is not new despite the Church's attempts to ignore, condemn, assimilate, or suppress it. Baptisms are a typical example of popular religion, pressure coming from the older generation to have their grandchildren "done" in a church. There were long-held beliefs that unless a baby had been baptized it would remain outside God's protective power, and that the Church might even forbid its burial in a churchyard, as had sometimes happened in times past.

No matter that young women have no Christian faith, they still seek to have their babies baptized. With marriages becoming increasingly rare, this can take the place of a wedding celebration for single girls. It gives them social standing as mothers and provides a ritual reinforcement of a family network. The demand in The Clarences was so great that the Loreto Sisters devised a popular service for the blessing of babies as an acceptable alternative rite. This sacrament was important as much for the cherishing of children as for a celebration of the community's future. Being a scion of a Kingdom community is infinitely more pleasing in the eyes of God than being a registered and card-carrying member of a church community.

Those who have rejected Christianity or do not believe in religion turn to spiritualism as another means of finding solace. In this belief system people seek to establish contact with the spirits of their dear departed ones, especially through a psychic medium. It was a popular way of coping with bereavement in The Clarences, as it was elsewhere in the North East.

The image that the Sisters used regularly themselves, resonating with the spirituality of Mary Ward, was the Rublev icon of the Trinity. They meditated on "how it illustrated the expression of community, and the focus on Jesus to which all eyes were turned". Another image, which they used in their prayers and Mass leaflets, was that of "The Transfiguration of Jesus" by the fifteenth-century artist Theophanes the Greek. As Imelda recalled: "Through these images the sheer beauty and awesome wonder before God was present as we were daily involved in the mystery and wonder of mission in The Clarences."[66]

In conversations with the Clarence residents, God frequently came into their discussions with remarks like, "I pray to God, you know", "When the chips are down you sense somehow there is a God", "I pray to God when I am frightened or desperate." Questions also surfaced, like "Where is God in all this pain and suffering?" The Sisters concluded that, although some people were regular in their prayers, most only prayed when times were hard or when they were in some sort of trouble. As one man said: "When I need God he will be there and I will go and tell him my troubles. But while everything is going fine I don't need him."

During my time, a survey was done by parishioners in a deprived estate in nearby Stockton-on-Tees on how the people there saw God. This compares well with The Clarences. Although many people in Stockton expressed a belief in God, they more usually would only call upon him in times of crisis. As a Stockton friend explained, he was a panic-button God: "When you push the panic-button he is expected to jump forward. No problem. I'll sort all this out. I'll do this and that to make things right. After the panic is over they shove him back in the cupboard and say thank you very much. Next time I need you I'll give you a call." The prevailing belief was that in times of trouble God would send someone to sort things out and fix the problem. In the meantime, the cross-in-my-pocket spirituality provided comfort and safe-keeping in daily life.

The Sisters' ministry of befriending enabled them to move from evangelization to the formation of a small worshipping group. This met regularly in their house, as did a weekly prayer club for children and young people. Hymn-singing was a favourite, but there were also drama, bible readings, a psalm, and prayers. A soft drink and biscuits afterwards made it a social occasion. Children often came to the door saying: "Give us a prayer miss", before going happily on their way.

House groups were another innovation, bringing adult Christians together for prayer, reflection, and discussion based on Scripture. Initially, they lacked confidence in articulating their faith, but as the groups grew, so did their convictions. The discussions were life-centred, focusing on immediate issues. This allowed members to express their faith freely and to relate it to their daily lives. After one Lent course, their biblical reflections led them to take action on behalf of the homeless, linking up with the housing officer in Stockton. Requests for baptisms also increased. At Christmas, they would go around the streets singing carols and the children loved it. On Good Friday, they walked around the estate with a cross.

The Sisters' idea of mission was not about converting people into becoming members of a church. It was a ministry of listening and of presence, a ministry of proclaiming Christ by incarnating him in all that they did and were. They also devised their own prayer card for the estate. They used a modern prayer with Celtic roots, with an image of the Transporter Bridge. It took pride of place in most homes.

Figure 11: The Transporter Bridge (Robert Cooper)

Poem Prayer

Be a bridge, Jesus
for the forgotten ones;
who nurture each other,
even as they struggle
to walk in your steps

Be a bridge, Jesus
between young and old,
frail and hardy;
gather us together
as your pilgrim people

The Revd Jay Kothare[67]

CHAPTER 6

Mission From Below

The mission of the Church is about discerning what the crucified God has already done and continues to do to incarnate the Kingdom in the world, and to participate by word, deed, and presence in this quest. This involves making visible the invisible grace of God in loving relationships, reconciliation, compassion, and justice. It also involves hallowing the structures of the world so that they become channels of the grace of God to the people of God. The Church needs to resist the temptation to disengage from the fractured world around it, but rather accept its challenges and so become a transforming, rather than a conforming, Church. The wounded world is a living reminder to the Church of the ever-present cross of Christ in our midst. The Church, for its part, should continue to serve and heal the crucified world. When the two are in such a symbiotic relationship we have the Kingdom. There is no gospel without the Kingdom, and no Kingdom without the cross.

Alas, a clerically orchestrated spirituality all too often tends to trickle down from above. It is dictated by dogma, doctrine, theology, and church polity, and is enforced through the hegemony of the Church. It is grounded in the expertise of professional theologians and may focus on Christ's divinity at the expense of his humanity. Such a spirituality feeds into mission from above and is dispensed by a hierarchy of clergy with varying degrees of power.

A people's spirituality bubbles up from below. It is a spirituality by the people, of the people, for the people, and embraces all cultures, creeds, denominations, and ethnicities. It arises from their day-to-day struggle to bring up a family, earn a living, or just survive on a meagre income, and needs to be treated with dignity and respect. As in The Clarences, it is inspired by the people's own experience of the divine, which they encounter in the world around them. Though springing from a people's powerlessness, yet it is empowering as it has no need to be endorsed by the Church or any other authority. It is rooted in a theology done by the people themselves, not necessarily learned, and seeks justice, peace, and the Kingdom here and now, rather than in heaven above, as promised by the sacrosanct creeds of the Church. Such a spirituality realistically affirms the humanity of Jesus, which is experienced at first hand, without denying his divinity. It is a spirituality that inspires mission from below.

Mission from above is conceived and carried out by specialists with minimal input from those at the receiving end. It is a top-down process informed by a theology from above, with its specialized expertise in terms of language, liturgy, catechism, and structures. At best, it would be concerned about reforming a certain situation, like trying to bring those outside the Church (the "un-churched") on board as card-carrying members, enhancing Church growth (more "bums on seats"), turning declining or dying churches around, or returning the disaffected back to the fold. Bright new packaging, persuasive literature, workshops, and directives from the hierarchy will be used to try to generate conformity and enthusiasm for a new mission strategy that promises much, but the *status quo* in society will remain largely unchallenged and unchanged.

Mission from above is likely to be sympathetic and patronizing, following the latest fashion in a one-size-fits-all designer programme. However inspired, it has to accommodate vastly different mission situations and will probably be couched in terms beyond the understanding of most people. Church groups will be at different stages in their journeys too. Some will be suffering from initiative fatigue. Others may have satisfactory long-term programmes already in place. Many more will be battling against the odds, or even quietly dying. Undue pressure to conform in any such situation will be counter-productive, if not downright frustrating to all concerned. Those who resent hierarchical interference are likely to offer dogged resistance.[68]

Another difficulty is the chronic dependency of many lay people on their clergy. This is a learned helplessness that remains deeply entrenched, even when the Church itself is no longer physically present, as in The

Clarences. Such long-term conditioning militates against independent initiatives in thought and action. It is even harder to penetrate when the laity believe that the only way to God is through a priest or minister, who is thought to guard the gates of heaven. This mindset sustains endemic conservatism and colludes with clergy domination in the "father knows best" school of theology.

The fact that too many clergy have become imprisoned within the precise formulations of systematic theology and doctrinal orthodoxy does not help. It is bad enough that their erudite preaching may well pass over the heads of their flock. But this obfuscation of theology also reinforces the low esteem of the listeners in the pews, as well as failing to address their immediate worries and concerns.

Laurie Green, a Church of England bishop, cites graffiti on a theological college wall as an example of just how intimidating this cerebral approach can be: "Jesus said to them, 'Who do you say that I am?' They replied, 'You are the eschatological manifestation of the ground of our being, in which kerygma we find the ultimate meaning in our interpersonal relationships.' And Jesus replied, 'What?'"[69] This is not to denigrate those faithful clergy who, year after year, humbly and lovingly feed their flock with profound but simple gospel truths, a lifetime of pastoral wisdom, and imaginative stories to bring their message alive.

Mission from above takes no cognizance of creative initiatives struggling to blossom from below, just waiting to be given the go-ahead in the local setting. What is needed is a missionary engagement that critiques both the positive and negative aspects of popular religion, but still gives people the freedom and encouragement to do their own local, contextual theology. This arises out of a particular context and addresses the needs and concerns of that context.[70]

The Bible is a prime example of a contextual record. God's acts of redemption and liberation are recorded in the Scriptures, long after they supposedly happened, from the different perspectives of those involved in the God-human covenant. In drawing on their unique experiences and memories of Jesus, the four Gospel writers are doing contextual theology when the different ways in which they choose to tell the same basic story would bring his message alive to their different constituencies.

In fact, all theologies are contextual whether this is acknowledged or not, since all theological thinking is determined by the immediate context of those engaged in the doing of theology. However, contextual theology per se implies "the *conscious* attempt to do theology from within the context of real life in the world".[71] It is a way of doing theology that is usually done communally and starts with a recording of a people's experiences and concerns.

Albert Nolan, a Dominican theologian from South Africa, argues that "any practising Christian can do theology . . . all that is necessary is an active faith". For him, "theology has for too long been an abstract study reserved for academic experts—producing a systemisation of answers to questions we no longer ask or at most an adaptation of answers to past questions which must now serve as a reservoir for answers to today's questions".[72] Speaking out of his experience as a parish priest in inner-city London, John Pridmore reiterated: "The only theology that is any use is theology born out of human need, not theology prepared in aseptic isolation and then applied like Elastoplast. Theology comes to life when it is shaped by what people . . . actually care about".[73]

Nolan goes on to say: "Different people in different parts of the world will ask different questions about faith according to their different historical, social, economic, political and cultural contexts. This will give rise to different theologies".[74] For him, this does not deny the fact that faith as a commitment to God in Jesus Christ remains the same at all times and in all circumstances. In other words, while there is one faith there are different theologies. They have acquired a range of names to reflect the diversity of their contexts, such as liberation theology in Latin America, black political theology in South Africa and the USA, African theology in its cultural form, feminist theology in the West, Dalit theology in India, Water Buffalo theology in Thailand, and many more.

In Jesus, God came down to live among us, not as a high and mighty king, but as one of the lowly who experiences the bitterest reality in our suffering world. When contextual theology is done among the poor, the disadvantaged, and the marginalized, they reinterpret the gospel from the underside of society. Mission from below then emerges from a theology from below. It aims to transform the unjust situation of a crucified community by proclaiming, praying, and working for the

Kingdom. Mission from above bears witness to the pain of God in Christ two thousand years ago. Mission from below bears witness to the pain of Christ suffering in and through people in the midst of a community here and now, and is totally committed to real-life situations.

Cross-shaped mission, as we would call it, is a grassroots movement, which generates its own motivation and momentum in an ongoing, ever-changing process, unique to the life of a particular community. It is energized by the idea that the people's concerns, needs, and resources are specific to its local context and culture. It is they who have to discern what God is already doing in the world around them and see how they can join in. It is they who identify their own priorities for mission and evangelism, and plan their own strategies, independent of interference or coercion from above, i.e. State and Church.

When a mission theology is owned by the people, then everything is viewed and judged from the vantage position of the foot of the cross, where they find power in their weakness and wisdom in their folly. Their Christian witness will thus be authentic as everything about them, be it prayer, meditation, liturgy, sacraments, evangelism, mission, theological thinking, fellowship, celebration, or the sharing of food, will be carried out in the shadow of the cross.

In this model of mission, a community needs to reflect on its own story and relate it to the story and narrative in the Bible. The local story must include all segments of the community. This kind of bible study would provide the necessary openness to listen to the still, small voice of the Holy Spirit as well as to the muted voices of our companions in our midst. In our bible study, we first listen to God as revealed in the scripture and then come back and listen to our neighbour. Finally, we funnel our collective grievances to God's mercy.

As Archbishop Desmond Tutu has said, we must follow Jesus' own example in which "disengagement, and waiting on God, precedes engagement". According to Tutu, an authentic spirituality of transformation requires that we must first spend time with Jesus in the wilderness before we can start dealing with issues of justice, peace, and reconciliation. Then we need to take the suffering of our wounded world back to God in prayer and contemplation in an ongoing two-way process.[75]

Strategies to initiate change or growth, or to confront unjust situations, however modest, will be a natural outcome of waiting on God. The community takes responsibility for its own decisions in setting goals, tries to incorporate the diversity of its constituency, takes any criticisms seriously, is open to change, works at its own speed, and is accountable to no one but itself for both its successes and its failures. By starting with easily realized projects, its members are encouraged to be more adventurous the second time around. As they grow in confidence they will advance from strength to strength and learn what works for them.

This process is independent of centralized directives, but help from advisers is welcomed where needed. Clearly there is a danger that, because we are advocating a grassroots theology that invites people to begin with their own experience, this may lead to a simplistic and uncritical use of the Bible. It may even be vulnerable to the syncretistic incorporation of negative aspects of folk beliefs. This is where professional theologians sympathetic to the process can help develop the necessary exegetical expertise among the laity, and offer the gift of their theological scholarship without disempowering the people involved. The advisers should also show themselves willing to be open to the insights of the people they are assisting, and sensitive to the way these are expressed.

On a visit to The Clarences in October 2015, local women told us how they had felt free to knock on the Sisters' door with any problem, knowing that they would be listened to with infinite patience and treated with the greatest respect: "When you needed spiritual comfort to give you a lift the Sisters would give you some as well as practical support. They didn't push religion down your throat. You could speak how you wanted to speak. One felt very comfortable with them. They gave me pride, hope, and courage to keep going and to fight for what I believed to be true."

We cannot better end this chapter than by quoting the IBVM (Loreto) order's Mission Statement: "We believe that every human being who is empowered to develop to one's best potential, proclaims the Glory of God. We see this empowerment as the distinguishing feature of all our efforts and the special thrust of our institute is to cherish a preferential love of the poor which is lived out both in our attitudes and structures."[76] There cannot be a finer statement on the convergence of theology, folk spirituality, and mission from below.

Reflection

Kingdom people seek first the Kingdom of God and its justice;
Church people often put church work above
    concerns of justice, mercy and truth.
Church people think about how to get people into the church;
Kingdom people think how to get the church into the world.
Church people worry that the world might change the church;
Kingdom people pray that the church is challenged
    and evangelized by the people of the world.

Based on a Youth Mission Prayer,
Christian Conference of Asia (no date).

CHAPTER 7

Walking Alongside the People

For the Clarence residents, the loss of all their places of worship had heightened their sense of deprivation and neglect. Even when people do not attend church, the building is a visible sign of a community's identity and sense of belonging. Many years previously, the Roman Catholic church had been the last to be demolished. After that the community felt that it had lost its centre. The people were now left without a place for communal rites of passage such as baptisms, confirmations, weddings, and funerals, as well as social and other gatherings. The Catholics retained a church presence by using people's homes as Mass centres until the community centre became available. Ministers from the Methodist, United Reformed, and Anglican churches had also held occasional services in the community centre until it, too, was closed after Stockton Borough Council was unable to pay for its upkeep.

With the coming of the Sisters, regular ecumenical worship took place either in their home or out on the street, weather permitting. There was a large, open grass space across the road from the Sisters' house, which could accommodate any overflow. These informal services had the support of the other denominations. On special occasions and for seasonal acts of worship, open-air services were the norm so as to accommodate larger numbers. Eventually, the refurbished Enterprise Centre became available and once again the community was able to come together under one roof. The turnout for the Sunday services became increasingly impressive. The people loved singing hymns from an almost forgotten past, the communal praise lifting them up to God. The Sisters also found that the power of symbols was significant, as in the breaking of bread, the lighting of candles, and the use of water, oil, and ashes.

The ecumenical ministers' group became a corporate mission unit, meeting monthly for prayer and reflection in the Sisters' home. They dealt with common issues such as how to contextualize the language of worship so that it became more meaningful to the residents.[77] The fraternal, ministerial fellowship provided an invaluable support network for the Sisters. Links with the industrial chaplain helped them gain an insight into the excessive rate of unemployment in The Clarences. This helped them ascertain what their role might be in trying to improve the situation. They also joined an inter-faith regeneration group for the Middlesbrough/Teesside area, which was developing projects for neighbourhood renewal. A multi-faith protest against the Iraq War was effective in building up wider community relationships, as was their participation in the Peace March in London in 2003.

One of the biggest difficulties for marginalized people is to get their voices heard by those in authority in an attempt to bring about change. The situation was aggravated by major cut-backs in government funding. This meant that borough councils like Stockton-on-Tees had limited available resources to meet the myriad claims for assistance. Residents in The Clarences had tried embarking on a campaign to alleviate their difficulties, but it was short-lived and had failed to achieve any positive outcomes. They lacked the necessary expertise, sustained support, and drive to make a successful impact.

What soon became apparent was the need for Imelda and Philippa to forge links with a whole range of public bodies outside the Church. Areas of particular concern related to the provision of health services, public transport, family support, youth work, community development, and industrial pollution. Such was the toxic air pollution that a neighbour's grass lawn died overnight, while washing hung out to dry could soon be covered with black soot.

The Sisters realized that sustainable improvement could only be achieved by working with various statutory, voluntary, and independent agencies. The challenge was to get a cynical community, accustomed to being relegated to the scrapheap, to co-operate with these groups. Perseverance was finally rewarded with partnerships that were either strengthened or, more usually, newly established. This gave the locals access to a wide range of regeneration programmes and resources, which previously had been quite beyond their reach.

For the Sisters, creating partnerships with members of the county and local councils, health professionals, and the police meant working together with officialdom as well as with the Clarence community. It also meant cutting through a minefield of red tape and bureaucracy in order to support the community's demands for better service deliveries. This entailed compiling and presenting a mass of evidence at a never-ending succession of meetings, which was both time-consuming and exhausting.

Short-term government funding and the constant turnover of community workers prevented any sustained action by the social services. However, because Imelda and Philippa lived permanently on the estate, they were never regarded as government agents constrained by time frames for projects and contracts. Nor was their ministry ever subservient to budgets, outcomes, and exit strategies, as were their counterparts in the field. Instead, by winning the community's trust they were treated as friends, neighbours, and readily available resource people—as one of their own. Because the people came first, the Sisters' focus was on spiritual nourishment, pastoral care, and social justice issues. Their involvement in collective action was always in a supportive role, working alongside the community rather than leading from up front as was more usually the case in secular and religious circles. This required patience, prayer, and persistence.

Networking paid off handsomely when community issues came under discussion. By establishing good relations with various authorities and public agencies, the Sisters made sure that The Clarences remained a priority on local government agendas. They were thus able to gain access to every possible source of funding and professional assistance. At the same time, the residents began to take concerted action themselves. Not only did they gather evidence on a whole range of problem areas, but as they gained in confidence they drew on their own experience in tackling the authorities and refused to be mollified by empty promises.

Public meetings were held in the High Clarence Primary School hall. These were widely advertised across the estate with posters and flyers. Once the residents realized that they had the upper hand, they packed the hall, with standing room only, and were vociferous in having their say. The council's representatives would deliver their reports expecting the usual apathetic acquiescence to decisions made from on high. Now they were forced to listen to a deluge of complaints and demands. They were clearly shocked at being confronted by a barrage of penetrating questions backed by well-researched information, and became defensive. However, the locals had no intention of being dumped yet again into the dustbin of officialdom, and could not be deterred in standing up for their rights.

I attended some lively meetings at which knowledgeable residents engaged in a spirited debate with the council's minions. The older generation provided a wealth of wisdom and experience, while the younger crowd added humour and energy. Despite their anger at the raw deal that had been dealt them over so many decades, the meetings were surprisingly good-humoured. Wisecracks from the audience were greeted with cheers and roars of laughter. The bantering helped to defuse rising tension and occasional outbursts of temper. The council officials had to contend with remarks like: "To you Port Clarence is a pain in the backside. How many more years of yapping will there be before action is actually taken?" This was loudly applauded and supported by others in a similar vein.

In many socially deprived estates competing for scarce resources, local councils were accustomed to making major decisions with minimal consultation. They might be required by law to engage in constructive discussions with grassroots communities, but mutual participation was often an illusion. In The Clarences, it was evident that public officials were accustomed to delivering sophisticated PowerPoint presentations supported by an impressive display of charts with an incomprehensible array of facts and figures. They might deign to answer a few questions, but would overrule any serious discussion before announcing their findings. But the residents had finally found their voice and, cheered on by their mates, could not be silenced.

The sudden shift in the balance of power was a daunting experience for the officials. They were left embarrassed and defenceless, slinking away from the meetings as soon as they possibly could. Signed petitions were also presented demanding immediate action on the most pressing problems. These demanded publicly planned procedures within a fixed timescale and could not easily be filed away and ignored.

At another meeting, the officials proudly presented ambitious plans for developing the Teesside National Nature Reserve, a former empty wasteland backing on to The Clarences. This was to become an extensive coastal reserve on the north and south banks of the Tees. The designated area had a wide range of wildlife habitats involving inter-tidal mud flats, sand dunes, small stretches of open water, and salt and grazing marshes. This was home to a large, internationally renowned variety of water and wading birds. It also included Seal Sands, host to the only regular breeding colony of common seals on the north-east coast. More than a thousand seals could commonly be seen basking in the tidal channels and on the sandbanks.[78]

One man, a plasterer by trade, drew a resounding response to this report when he protested that, exciting as the proposed nature reserve might be, the authorities seemed to care more about preserving bird life than about suffering people close by. This was at a time when an unattended blocked culvert had caused serious flooding across the estate; a rat infestation in huge heaps of uncollected rotting rubbish had become a health hazard; uncontrolled fly-tipping was turning the place into a garbage dump; industrial pollution was causing chronic illness among young and old; and the high rates of unemployment and poverty were desperate facts of daily life. The officials were forced to take note as these issues were reeled off one by one and were supported by an appreciative audience. Some of the accents were hard to follow, but the explicit descriptions left nothing to the imagination.

Although the Sisters were always present in a supportive role, they were not above stirring the pot. One woman later related her experience in attending a seminar led by a so-called expert on drugs. It soon became apparent that the speaker did not have a clue about the effect of drug abuse on family life. After insistent prodding by Imelda, who was not about to let the opportunity pass by, my informant was forced into summoning up the courage to talk about her own experience in dealing with her son's addiction. As she told the speaker: "You don't know what you are talking about. You haven't been through it like me and others like me sitting here." It had been a long haul to get the boy off drugs, but the Sisters had helped by organizing a rehabilitation programme.

At the start of the Sisters' ministry, Fr Austin Smith had advised them that, in order for a disadvantaged community to move out of powerlessness, they needed to forge strong links with the middle class if they wished to effect radical change. He believed that broad-based organizing in solidarity with the poor could only be achieved by changing the consciousness of the middle class. The institutional Church was the most obvious insertion point, and local churches from outside the estate provided such support.

Some, like an ecumenical association in a village nearby, and the Roman Catholic members of the Society of St Vincent de Paul,[79] became an active and dynamic presence in The Clarences. As Imelda said, "The poor and the rich sat down regularly together and we marvelled at the friendships which were made. It was a true gospel experience".[80] The Sisters also founded a Mary Ward affiliate programme. This involved a number of lay people who felt called to work in a ministry on the margins of society while being closely associated with a religious order.

Imelda and Philippa were much influenced in their work by the Jesuit theologian, Jon Sobrino. Spanish-born, he has spent most of his life teaching in El Salvador and has been a leading figure in the Liberation Theology movement in Latin America. His theology has been criticized by some for focusing too much on the human nature of Jesus at the expense of Christ's divinity. But he has remained committed to helping the world's poor and oppressed. When interviewed recently, he said that "practically [they are] of no consequence to anyone—not to the people who live in abundance nor to the people who have any kind of power". He maintained that "there is a reality of sin, which has structural causes and kills a majority of the population". There was an evident need to overcome this situation for "without doing this task theology was neither human nor Christian". As he continued:

> From here I re-thought the reign of God—as justice and fellowship—as the core of Jesus of Nazareth. I re-thought the historical Jesus and the following of him, including centrally his compassion towards the poor, the announcement of the good

news to the oppressed and the denunciation of the oppressors
... For this he died on a cross ... the risen Christ is a crucified
Christ. The resurrection of Jesus was the reaction of God against
the victimizers who killed the innocent. From the love of the
crucified and from his rehabilitation on the part of God emerges
hope. God is the God of life in a struggle against the idols that
demand death for their survival.[81]

In his book, *Spirituality of Liberation: Toward Political Holiness,* he
stresses the importance of being honest with reality and being faithful
to it.[82] This was a significant influence on the Sisters' mission in The
Clarences, ensuring that they stayed in touch with real-life situations as
opposed to the prevailing myths churned out by the media. It also meant
that they remained in partnership with the people rather than being
tempted to take charge.

At the same time, although the Sisters imbibed a lot of Sobrino's
missionary zeal, they tempered and deepened it with the discipline of
prayer and contemplation. This dimension is often muted in Liberation
Theology. Undoubtedly the Sisters had an unspoken loyalty and closeness
to Roman Catholic doctrine, and were bound by allegiance to Rome.
Nonetheless, they kept clerical influence to the minimum and even struck
an interdenominational, secular chord in their overall ministry. In this
they bravely but unobtrusively imitated the pioneering example set by
Mary Ward herself centuries earlier.

Meditation

Christ Has No Body—St Teresa of Avila (1515–1582)

Christ has no body but yours,
no hands, no feet on earth but yours,
yours are the eyes with which he looks with
compassion on this world.
Yours are the feet with which he walks to do good.
Yours are the hands with which he blesses all the world.
Yours are the hands, yours are the feet,
yours are the eyes, you are his body.

The Bookmark of St Teresa of Avila

Let nothing disturb you,
let nothing frighten you,
lll things are passing;
God never changes.
Patience obtains all things.
Whoever has God lacks nothing.
God alone suffices.

This prayer composed by the Carmelite nun derives its name from the tradition that she carried it around in her prayer book, where it was found after her death.[83]

CHAPTER 8

Empowering Action

When Thomas Merton, the Trappist monk and mystic, discussed meditation with the Dalai Lama, the single question that exercised his mind was: "How can the refined consciousness achieved through meditation be harnessed to generate action that would transform people's lives?" For Merton, Christian meditation was not an end in itself, but a means to bring about the Kingdom.[84]

True Christian meditation must manifest itself outwardly in self-effacing works, which fulfil one's faith (cf. James 2. 22). This inward quality embraces, among others, things like silence, prayer, faith, meditation, listening, watching, and waiting on God, as well as an analytical sensitivity to the pain of the people of God. Any action that arises out of this inner preparedness can move mountains and help usher in the Kingdom. When the disciples asked Jesus why their tireless deeds were not sufficiently effective, he reminded them that their work lacked an inward quality (cf. Matthew 17. 19–21).[85]

The Church has always prided itself on serving the crucified Lord in the guise of the poor, God being revealed in the poverty of Jesus. The debate arises over the way in which this Christian love is manifested. Traditionally, the faithful have followed the Good Samaritan model through charity and good works—feeding the hungry, clothing the naked, comforting the bereaved, housing the homeless, and tending the sick, the elderly, and the disabled. Well and good. The problem is that this model only seeks to dispense loving service by trying to patch up a needy situation without touching the root causes of that need.

There is the story of the baroness who went around the country demonstrating twenty different ways to cook a cod's head to working-class women. One night she was floored when asked, "What has happened to the rest of the cod?" Like the baroness, we may have the best intentions as Christians to do good works, but in our enthusiasm it is so easy to become patronizing, or even to try and control those less fortunate than ourselves. Ultimately, we are so busy being Good Samaritans, however worthy, that we fail to challenge unjust situations.

Laurie Green, now retired as a bishop, issues just such a challenge in his recent book, *Blessed are the Poor? Urban Poverty and the Church*.[86] Speaking from his own experience in the East End of London, he raises searching questions: "Where are the poor in Britain today?", "Who or what has impoverished them?", "How can they be a blessing to the world?" According to Green, the excluded and the marginalized are mostly found on poor housing estates. In this lost world of a working-class culture, a diminishing manufacturing base and government policies on benefits have destroyed all hope of a better life. Those at the bottom of the heap may even be blamed for their impoverishment. For Green, the Church should be poor and for the poor. It needs to free itself from the trappings that stop it engaging in effective mission. The residents of poor estates need to be listened to, engaged with, and valued for who they are and for what they can do—not what the institutions can do for them—so that the effective, life-enhancing, and radical change can allow the poor to be a blessing.

One of the best ways of generating community action is to join forces with an established pressure group that has the wherewithal to initiate projects and mount a campaign. Church Action on Poverty (CAP) is one such group. CAP is an ecumenical Christian social justice charity dedicated to challenging the root causes of poverty in the UK. Not believing in an ambulance ministry, its vision is to create a fairer society by narrowing the gap between rich and poor. It works in partnership with churches and with the people concerned to find solutions to poverty locally, nationally, and internationally.[87]

The Teesside CAP group met monthly in the Sisters' home at Port Clarence. A national initiative in which it first became involved was in helping to organize a "Hearing on Poverty" in the Teesside area during the 1990s. Key speakers were people with a direct experience of poverty but who seldom, if ever, got the chance to speak publicly and be heard. As David Cross, a member of Teesside CAP and previously unemployed, said: "It's about listening, listening to those who are often talked at, who have decisions made for them, and have things done for them, but don't often get the chance to speak for themselves. They can speak for themselves if given the opportunity. Listen to them and allow them to challenge us."[88]

At the Hearing, a woman spoke of how the Department of Social Services had threatened to cut her benefits if she did more than a few hours of voluntary work every week, as she would no longer be actively seeking employment. A single parent explained that, in the present economic system, money was supposed to trickle down to the poor. But Margaret Thatcher's policy was far from the truth. The poor actually lived in fear of losing what little they had. This woman pleaded for generosity to trickle down instead of greed, for hope to trickle down instead of suicidal hopelessness.

Among other speakers were a man made redundant and now long-term unemployed, a disabled man, and a pensioner. The latter quoted St Ambrose in saying, "You are not making a gift of what is yours to the poor man but you are giving him back what is his . . . The earth belongs to everyone." A common theme was the need for the human spirit to do something that has a purpose, a meaning in life. "We are not disposable assets as in the system," asserted one woman, "we are human beings."

All spoke passionately from the heart, from their own experience. Many broke down in tears. Although a final report was published, nothing came of it. Nothing changed. Those on the underside of society continued to live in fear of an oppressive system that meted out punishment to anyone who dared to protest or offer any sort of challenge. One man I knew had his benefits cut when he had the temerity to lodge a complaint about an administrative fault that had docked his meagre dole money.

Act See

Pray Judge

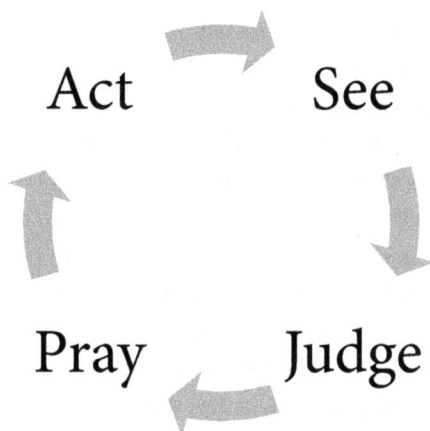

Figure 12: Diagram of the Pastoral Cycle

The Teesside CAP group consisted of five Roman Catholics (the nuns being resident), one Anglican (myself), a Quaker couple, and a number of local women. We used the Pastoral Cycle—the See-Judge-Act method of social analysis, theological reflection, and planning for action—as our model. This helped us to clarify our objectives and determine our way forward. David Cross, from Middlesbrough, now working for CAP and a member of our group, had studied this method and took the lead. I was familiar with it too as it was in common usage in South Africa.[89]

The Pastoral Cycle begins with the context of a real-life situation, a concrete reality, rather than some abstract concept. The participants draw on their own way of thinking about God, and their personal Christian practices. They are not interested in what theologians have to say about the Church, like "the glorious bride of Christ", or something in a similar vein. Rather, as Nolan so cogently argues, there is an implicit and instinctive faith within people's everyday experience. Anybody can do theology if they have an active faith. "This faith might need to be verbalised and analysed and criticised but it is the real faith of the people who are trying to understand as opposed to the ideal faith that so many theologians talk about but never experience."[90]

The next step in the cycle is to bring together a group of people to reflect on a specific issue of injustice in their community. They must be an integral part of the consultation process from the start. It is their grievances that are being addressed and it is their experience that provides the motivation for pursuing the issue. Mission from below now moves into action. Factual information about the chosen project is then collected and collated so that it can be analysed in detail. This may need considerable research in covering a wide range of data and must be done with meticulous care. Schematic diagrams are helpful in identifying the key factors at stake, as is a map of the chosen area to be covered.[91]

With sufficient information at hand, the group proceeds to ask penetrating questions. These delve deep into the workings of the systems and structures that allow the injustice to persist. Resources play an important part in the process, whether they are historical, sociological, economic, political, or biblical. Experts in a particular field can be consulted, but their contribution must be targeted at the issues at stake.

Once the analysis is complete, the cycle moves on to prayer and theological reflection. Bible studies are a common pursuit in British churches, but they are an end in themselves and seldom lead to any positive action. In this method, biblical texts are chosen that provide insight and teaching from the Gospels, enabling the group to do its own theology and to draw practical conclusions. Finally, a plan of action is decided upon. Both short-term and long-term goals may need to be clarified, together with a fixed timescale. This ensures accountability in achieving specific objectives. The "who, why, what, when, and how" questions are a key component, as is the need to sustain interest with regular report-backs.

Members of the group are given different tasks, sharing in an appropriate plan of action. As many local people as possible are invited to participate because they have the requisite knowledge and need to own the process from start to finish. The results of a typical campaign are collected, collated, and presented in a documented form. The nuclear group is then able to analyse their findings to see what further steps might need to be taken, and to identify other injustices that have surfaced in the course of the survey. The sharing of experiences can provide much laughter as well as sorrow at the burdens some people have to bear.

In planning any sort of action, care must be taken to distinguish between feverish activism and Christian discipleship. In too many churches the faithful few are landed with the burden of any new mission work. After the energy of these charitable souls has been dispersed in innumerable directions, it is no wonder that they are invariably left exhausted and dispirited with meagre results. They will then say, "We have tried that and it didn't work", as I know to my cost. Frenzied busyness may appear to be laudable, but it will be counter-productive if it only scratches the surface of a serious situation without addressing the deeper issues.

In following the Pastoral Cycle, focused action will involve the community as a whole; new leadership is encouraged from within their midst, while people of all ages and abilities will be given the chance to acquire new skills and to put these into practice. Teamwork is developed in achieving shared objectives, self-worth and self-confidence are gained in confronting what may seem like daunting challenges, and pride and self-respect are restored in bringing about change that will make a real difference in their neighbours' lives.

Our Teesside CAP group used the Pastoral Cycle to focus on the structural sin of injustice due to the absence of any fuel pay point in The Clarences. In our theological reflections, using Isaiah 61. 1–3, and Luke 1. 46–55 (the *Magnificat*) in particular, we felt that Christ was not content to call us only to proclaim the gospel and do good works, but also to act out our calling. We firmly believed that love is expressed through justice, and that justice must be lived out in action, not just in pious thoughts and deeds.

The residents themselves had identified fuel poverty as one of the most crippling injustices, which caused them the most suffering. Those who could afford to pay for their gas and electricity by direct debit received a discount. The majority, however, who paid cash to recharge their meters were doubly oppressed. They had to travel some four miles to the nearest pay point and were then charged higher rates. Added to which, public transport was unreliable and the return trip took nearly eighty minutes each way, costing about four pounds. All this expense and inconvenience to pay a fuel bill of perhaps ten pounds. Installing a pay point on the estate would enable them to recharge their keys on site. Yet repeated attempts to resolve the matter had been turned down by Stockton Borough Council. It claimed that a pay point would not be economically viable on such a poor estate.

Having earned the trust of the community over a number of years, our CAP group launched the campaign by holding a series of public meetings to gauge the locals' response. This was followed by a door-to-door survey devised by David Cross to measure the economic viability of the campaign. The residents were warned beforehand of our need to gather reliable information from the entire community to support the action, and to expect to be visited by the people carrying out the survey. Each CAP member was paired with at least one local woman, the estate was carved up into manageable entities, and almost every home was visited with the questionnaire.[92]

The Clarences is a tough environment and as we went from door to door my companion, who lived on her own, was extremely fearful of our reception. We might well have met with animosity and she could have been targeted for reprisals. We had to go after dark too, when people were more likely to be at home. It did not help that it was just before Christmas and the weather was bitterly cold, windy, and wet. Surprisingly, we were given an enthusiastic welcome as we worked our way down the streets, and were offered hospitality in many homes. Bright Christmas decorations added to the festive cheer. Only those few who could afford to pay by direct debit politely refused to fill out the questionnaire. What I found extremely depressing was the number of boarded-up houses in the locality and this was not peculiar to our designated area. Unlit, in poor repair, and overgrown with weeds, they looked cold and forbidding in the darkness.

The injustice of the situation was exemplified by one woman. She told us: "Someone has to take me to a pay point if my key runs out at night, otherwise I have no heating or means of preparing food. Not all that many people have cars either and they get fed up at having to come to my aid." Her neighbour was equally loquacious in venting her anger: "The government doesn't give a damn about the little people. We shouldn't have to say we are poverty-stricken to get our rights. It is degrading."

David Cross had the unenviable task of summarizing the questionnaires and drawing up the final report. The response to the survey was overwhelmingly positive, with 93 per cent in favour of action. The campaign also had the support of Frank Cook, the local MP, giving it extra clout. Within two months it achieved its goal. Stockton Borough Council agreed to site a pay point in the newly established Enterprise Centre in Port Clarence. Despite the Council's misgivings, it was in constant use and was soon paying its way.

Another initiative was in making effective use of the local and regional press. Regular reports were issued with accompanying photographs. This publicity was designed to hold the authorities to account in implementing promised action. The opening of an urban farm on the estate, where children could receive appropriate education, was one of the first success stories.

The residents felt that they, "the little people", had at last made their voices heard. Their action group was soon tackling a host of other issues, such as improved transport services, the prevention of regular flooding of houses and roads, the endemic pollution, and the use of toxic waste to repair their roads. The community was brought together in an entirely new way. As one woman commented: "We must avoid the danger of seeing ourselves at the bottom of the pile. Local people have a strong sense of community and are quite prepared to do things themselves for themselves." She had been involved in the pay point campaign and helped to initiate the other projects.

Theology from below is realized in mission when people are motivated to look outwards and are moved to help those who are even less fortunate than themselves. The Clarences' Residents' Action Group was only too willing to share its experience, and the extensive media coverage inspired other small communities to follow suit. New partnerships were established and there was no stopping them.

Reflection by St Catherine of Siena (1347–1380)

An extract from a letter to her Confessor

Build in your heart a prayer cell,
abide in the stable within,
and there be born,
again and again,
serving God's poor.

Contemplative Prayer attributed to St Brigid of Kildare, Ireland (*c*.453–*c*.521)

I arise today through a mighty strength;

God's power to guide me,

God's might to uphold me,

God's eyes to watch over me,

God's word to give me speech,

God's hand to guard me,

God's way to lie before me,

God's shield to shelter me,

God's host to secure me.

St Brigid's charism of hospitality

I long for a great lake of ale.

I long for the meals of faith and piety.

I long for the flails of penance at my house.

I long to give away jars brimming with love.

I long for them to have cellars full of mercy.

I long for cheerfulness to be in their drinking.

I long for Jesus to be there among them.

CHAPTER 9

Church Growth or Kingdom Growth?

Let us keep the peace of the gospel with one another,
and beyond us, with the rest of mankind.

St Hilda's last words to the sisters of
Whitby Abbey on her deathbed

As The Clarences entered into an irreversible economic downturn, the churches that had ministered to the community, some over many years, all left, leaving the residents high and dry. Ironically, just when the village most needed spiritual comfort and moral uplift, there was no Church presence. The Sisters eventually stepped into this vacuum, not representing any institutional church, but only as a listening presence imbued with the spirituality and vision of Mary Ward.

During their listening process, Imelda and Philippa identified health issues as one of the most pressing problems on the estate. Poverty goes together with high levels of stress, an inadequate diet, a lack of energy, and chronic ill health. In The Clarences, this was exacerbated by severe climatic conditions and noxious pollution from the chemical industry.

The incidence of stress-related illness, cancer, diabetes, and heart and respiratory disease was abnormally high, as were the premature mortality rates, while the people's quality of life was abysmal. Health provision was almost non-existent. The nearest medical facilities were at Billingham, a costly bus ride away, discouraging regular usage. A half-hearted attempt by the residents to rectify the situation with a visiting doctor had petered out.[93] The injustice of the situation became another urgent priority for communal action.

The founding of The Clarences Well-Being Project was a major joint venture inspired by the Sisters. This entailed a comprehensive health survey of the community, an evaluation of the findings to formalize the evidence, more public meetings, and much lobbying of the council authorities. The resurrection of the Enterprise Centre was the first step along the way. The original community centre had been closed due to economic stringencies. Later, the Teesside Development Corporation had provided funds for the new Enterprise Centre and this had become the focal point for community get-togethers. Run by the residents, however, the lack of professional skills and resources meant that it had offered little of value, except as a central meeting place, and had struggled to survive.

Energized by a sense of working together to achieve common goals and with renewed funding, the centre was closed for a time and totally refurbished. The residents were rewarded with a sparkling new health facility offering a wide range of medical and social services. The medical wing was staffed by a community nurse with all the necessary facilities. A relay of doctors attended on a part-time basis. Across the courtyard, the Community Hub boasted a welcoming receptionist, a well-stocked food co-operative, the fuel pay point, a post office, a prescription drug outlet, crèche facilities (Stay and Play), and a hairdresser. A thriving café provided a pleasant social venue with a tempting array of eats and refreshments.

After-school activities for children included kickboxing, dancing, arts and crafts, and drug prevention work. Adults were offered a variety of programmes ranging from stress and anger management to art, yoga, music therapy, digital photography, massage, advice on home furnishing, adult literacy and numeracy training, and a fully equipped computer suite. The adjoining Peace Centre was flanked by plants from people's gardens.

Professional help was given to train people and support the development of the centre's activities, and it received several prestigious awards. Copious press coverage was a huge boost to the community's self-esteem and pride in their achievements. An "Action for Jobs" team also began working on the estate. This helped to boost the number of people in employment as well as assisting the unemployed to make the best of their difficulties.

The Peace Centre and garden were the Sisters' special project. They had long felt the need for a quiet place on the estate where people could find refuge when they were under stress and needed a private place to grieve, reflect in silence, or just pray and be alone with God. The Centre was established with generous outside funding and offered facilities for a full-time counsellor, a family drug therapy unit, stress relief work, and meditation, as well as art, drama, and music. The Sisters used it for community worship, Sunday Masses with visiting priests, and the ritual passages of life such as the blessing of babies and memorial services. The Peace Garden was laid out around the courtyard. This enclosed space was ideal for large acts of worship, as well as dance and drama.

True to their Congregation's remit to be mobile and move on to new ministries, Imelda and Philippa finally left The Clarences in 2004 after sixteen years. By then, a Partnership Board had been established as a company with limited liability. This enabled them to raise funds as long as their projects remained viable. Continuity in the regeneration of the estate was also assured through strong new leadership, while a ministry team had taken over the responsibility of developing the Christian community.

Such a radical transformation does not happen overnight and all these positive developments took time. But for the patient perseverance of Imelda and Philippa, it is doubtful that anything much would have changed. Their mission was not to dictate, but to come alongside a grossly deprived and neglected community to empower the residents to take responsibility for challenging the many wrongs meted out to them and so improve their lives. Mary Ward's life of prayer, teaching, and a zeal for righteousness provided the blueprint for the Loreto Sisters' apostolic ministry of active service. Uniquely, they led without leading by allowing the people's latent leadership skills to emerge and flourish.

Led by a team of two redoubtable and independent women, this mission from below was silently subversive in confronting male models of priesthood and its jealously guarded hierarchies. With female clergy now in the ascendance, and female bishops being consecrated in the Church of England, things may well follow a new direction. It all depends on whether they are able to resist being co-opted into the historical structures of power, and whether they proactively facilitate the release of the laity's God-ordained potential from the perennial restraints of clergy control.

In establishing a ministry of presence among and alongside the poor and the marginalized, the Sisters' mission was about listening, comforting, sharing, consoling, counselling, and interceding. It was a ministry of binding the wounded together physically, emotionally, and spiritually, and allowing the community to grow in fellowship and learn to seek their own healing, wholeness, and justice without any undue interference from "experts". The Sisters steered clear of theological dogma and doctrine, and seldom imposed their own religious convictions upon people. There was no Bible-thumping and little emphasis was given to preaching. Silence is the best preaching in a mission of presence.

A non-sacramental populist liturgy, which the Sisters themselves designed, resonated with the people's cultural ethos and way of doing things. Giving them space to do their own theology with which to explore the teachings of the Gospels themselves, as among the first Christian communities, emboldened them to discover their own personal faith on their own terms and at their own pace. For the people of The Clarences, the lived revelation was that God had not only manifested himself in Jesus two thousand years ago, but that he was daily and actively present in their humdrum lives. This infused in them the spiritual militancy to take on and exorcise the demons of despair and exclusion that had haunted them for so long. In so doing, they were able to celebrate a new sense of pride and self-worth, and a new way of being a community. They were no longer a lost and forgotten people.

Under the Sisters, every believer became a priest with a stake in the destiny and mission of the estate. The people identified with, endorsed, and participated in their own mission from below without interference from any accredited missioner or clergyperson. In this sense, worship (derived from the old English *worth-ship*) became literally a channel and an event in and through which the people were inspired to rediscover their own worth as free thinking and feeling individuals. This had previously been suppressed by the institutional Church through its dogma and clergy-centred ritualism.

The worshipping fellowship accepted one and all—believers, non-believers, Christians of all shades, young and old, gay and straight, people of all faiths and none, the poor and not so poor. There was no church building, no pulpit, no collection of money, only a gathering place around the Peace Centre where they could worship together. They were without a formal liturgy—no creed, no sermon, no confession, no dogma, and no pressure to make any sort of binding commitment of belonging or declaration of faith. This was not only a challenge to the sectarian requirements of a mainstream Church, but also an appeal and an invitation to the wider society, which had lost faith in its Christ-given mission, to live up to Christ's commission to build a Kingdom where everyone was equal before God.

Here, for the sake of clarity as to what we have said about the Church, we need to briefly define what we mean. By Church we do not mean the invisible Body of Christ symbolizing the people of God, but the traditional, institutional, established Church with its hierarchy of male domination, dogma, ritualism, Eurocentrism, and apolitical ethics. This Church has consistently divided humanity between believers and unbelievers, saved and unsaved, Christian and non-Christian, lay and ordained, male and female, chosen and un-chosen, high-born and low-born. It dissects the world between the religious and the secular and claims to have a direct line of contact with God, which is the Church elite's theological rationale for their power over the laity.

At the time, Fresh Expressions of Church were becoming all the rage across the churches. It was seen as a creative way forward in reversing a rapid decline in the numbers of churchgoers and all this entailed—a critical drop in finances, the expensive upkeep of historic buildings with dwindling congregations, staffing issues, and so forth. Not surprisingly, the Sisters' pioneering ministry at The Clarences was seen by some as one more experiment in exploring new ways of being church, which it certainly was not.[94] A fresh expression of church is defined as:

> Any gathering or network that engages mainly with people who have never been to church, or who are not members of any church. There is no single model, but the emphasis is on starting something which is appropriate for its context, rather than cloning something that works elsewhere. The principles underlying this will be listening to people and entering their

context, serving those outside the church, incarnational mission, with the making of disciples a priority. It will have the potential to become a mature expression of church shaped by the Gospel and the enduring marks of the church and for its cultural context.[95]

There are now said to be over three thousand new forms of church across a broad range of denominations and traditions in the UK. Looking very different from a traditional church, their meeting places vary from village and school halls to coffee houses, cafés, pubs, businessmen's offices, skateboarding rinks, youth clubs, homes in old and new housing estates, and every sort of discarded premises from boarded-up shops and stores to old carpet factories and cotton mills. In order to mesh with the local culture, there might be smoking allowed during times of worship, drinks in a pub, tea and biscuits, or some activity for the young.

Their distinguishing features mean that they are not an old church with a new name, rebranded or refurbished, but an entirely new church in its own right. Nor are they "a bridge project to which people belong for a while before going to a 'proper church'". Some people do eventually choose to attend a more traditional church, or even keep a foot in both churches. The main objective, however, is:

> To work towards establishing a new community or congregation especially for those who have never been involved in church (un-churched) or once were, but left for whatever reason (de-churched). If, though, the intention is to do mission better or more imaginatively in order to attract people to an existing church, it isn't a fresh expression (although doing that is always an excellent idea).[96]

The multiplication of new churches meant that existing church structures had to be expanded to allow for some form of accountability within a legal framework. In the Anglican Church, pioneer ministers, lay and ordained, have been selected for this work. They must have the necessary vision and gifts to be "missionary entrepreneurs", to be able to "form and lead fresh expressions and new forms of church appropriate to a particular culture".[97]

Since 1999, there has been an outpouring of publications on fresh expressions of church, and a selection has been provided for further study.[98] A recent offering—*Ancient Faith, Future Mission: Fresh Expressions in the Sacramental Tradition*—is an anthology of writings from the catholic tradition. With their Tractarian model of serving poor communities, social uplift is a central feature of their missionary work. But in their theological reflections and case studies used to highlight a variety of new initiatives, Church growth remains a necessary premise and precondition to serving the Kingdom of God.[99] The Church is the handmaid of the Kingdom and without the Church there is no scope for the Kingdom to come into being.

The common theme in all this literature is that it is always about the Church doing things for the people of God. However, there is no concern for the will of the people as to what they seek for themselves or whether they might elect to do it themselves without having to look to the Church.

Case studies on "Growing the Church" follow a slightly different trajectory, but are in tandem with "fresh expressions". They usually begin with a statistical analysis, which monitors changes in membership in different sizes of church over a certain period of time. We are overwhelmed with figures in Bob Jackson's findings as to what makes a church grow, as opposed to those that are static or in decline. He includes missions with families and young people, prayer discipline, training leaders, inter-diocesan strategies, and multi-parish leadership. He also questions the future of the parish model and underlines the need to measure spiritual growth and vitality.[100]

But does Church growth necessarily involve Kingdom growth? Without a church, The Clarences would not even appear on any database and yet they have a strong sense of community with a staunch conviction of God's presence in their midst. It was the Church which left them, not they who left the Church. Yet the mission blossomed without any Church presence thanks to the secular initiatives brought in by the Sisters.

David Goodhew, who heads the Centre for Church Growth Research based at Cranmer Hall, in Durham, has edited a selection of essays which compare Church growth with secular and liberal theology.[101] Secularization is seen as a main cause of Church decline. But a wholesome secularization is the basis of the spirituality in The Clarences.

The secular and not the religious or the "churchy" is at the heart of the Incarnation. God became flesh to sanctify and transform the material world. The problem with the institutional Church is that it separates the religious from the secular in the name of Church growth at the expense of Kingdom growth. As disciples of the incarnate Son, we fully embrace the secular to transform the world so that all life, not just the host at the Lord's Table, may become a sacrament. The main cause of Church decline is not secularization but that the Church has become too religious and lost touch with the very material world which Jesus came to love and save.

The emphasis on numerical growth ignores the role played even by a static or declining church in providing an integrating focus or central meeting place in a small community, as in a rural village or deprived housing estate. The present trend is to bunch such churches together in pastoral teams, as has now lately happened at The Clarences. The rationale is that they will pool their resources and gifts. The object is to save money on clergy personnel and structures. One cleric may have charge of as many as ten churches spread over a large area, with all the time-consuming administration and oversight involved. Not only is this a back-breaking task, but it fails to value each community as an entity in itself with its particular history and unique sense of identity. Instead of seeking new ways of being church, we ought to focus on venturing new ways of being a community without having to label it as Christian or otherwise.

There is much work still to be done, in finding new ways of being a community, that has nothing to do with putting more bums on seats, or whether they are indigenous churches or not. What we do not need are inward-looking holy huddles peopled by activist do-gooders fired by a "let's-pray-for-the-poor" ethic. Rather, the question is whether so-called fresh expressions of church do indeed lead to a real transformation of communities and facilitate new ways of praying the Kingdom.

A Kingdom community, particularly among the poor, does not only pray for itself but does something about it. It does its own theology, designs its own liturgy (i.e. the work of the people), bears each other's crosses, seeks God for itself instead of through a representative of the Church, regards every little act as a sacrament, and includes all of God's creation in the scheme of redemption.

What Imelda and Philippa tried to do in The Clarences was to build up a Kingdom community. That is their legacy. The Health Centre involved both mental and physical healing. The Peace Centre garden provided environmental healing. Above all else, they brought the people together and restored their confidence in themselves. They gave them back the power and the initiative to run their lives as they wished. This gave them hope and a purpose.

United under God irrespective of race, religion, class, gender, age, or possessions, a Kingdom community is galvanized by spirituality rather than religiosity. First and foremost, what the people seek is not a Church or Church growth or new ways of being Church, but a community in transformation fulfilling the hopes and aspirations of the people without any dependency either on the State or the Church. The ethics of the community are spiritual, secular, cosmopolitan, and egalitarian.

Kingdom growth, as opposed to Church growth, glorifies Christ, who is the Lord of the Kingdom. If the traditional Church's vision of Jesus was as a Nordic, yellow-haired Aryan, then is it any surprise that the Church's vision of the Kingdom is equally shallow, limited, and non-inclusive? Christian discipleship is an unending process of putting on Christ, delving into the mind of Christ, unravelling the myriad dimensions we are heir to in Christ.

There are aspects of Christ's mercy we have been blind to. The poor of the non-western world opened our eyes as never before to see the social justice dimension of the Kingdom. Women from around the globe have taught us that the ascended Christ is both male and female, and in this Kingdom there is no sexual division. Indigenous peoples in Australasia, Africa, and the Americas have, through their nurturing of God's creation, shown us that the Kingdom embraces the redemption of man no more than of animals, trees, rivers, hills, and the earth itself. The sages of the East have opened up to us the immense possibilities of meditation and silent communion. All these traditions and spiritualities have a share in Christ's Kingdom. They should humble us enough to make us realize the vastness and profundity of the love and justice of Christ, and dedicate ourselves to the mission of Kingdom growth itself.

The "Rainbow of Humanity" Prayer

This was used in a typical act of worship led
by the Sisters at The Clarences.

Leader: Living God, you call us out of our separate flower-pots to bloom together in the multicoloured glory of your garden. Blessing you for your gifts of difference and colour, we pray:

Colour us red, passionate God, for the anger of the oppressed, for those who hunger and thirst for justice and peace, for all who labour to give birth to love.
All: Lord, have mercy.

Colour us yellow, resurrection God, for the achievements of the years, for those who light up our lives, for all who dwell in the shadows of death and long for the dawn of life.
All: Lord, have mercy.

Colour us green, creator God, for the integrity of creation, for seeds planted and leaves for the healing of communities and nations, for all who need a new way forward to grow.
All: Lord, have mercy.

Colour us blue, incarnate God, for all who weep, for faith to walk, and even dance on the water, for all who need heaven to be torn open that they may hear God's affirming word—"you are my daughter, my son, whom I love".
All: Lord, have mercy.

Colour me purple, holy God, for those whose needs and gifts are ignored, rejected: for the silenced who need a voice, and for the powerful who need to listen, for imagination and wisdom for us all.
All: Lord, have mercy.

CHAPTER 10

Banished out of the City Gates

To evoke the utter ignominy of Christ's death, the scripture tells us that in his final hours he was dragged beyond the Old City limits and crucified outside the City Gates. "Jesus suffered outside the gates to sanctify the people with his own blood. Let us go to him, then, outside the camp and bear his humiliation." (Hebrews 13. 12–13). This cursed place where the cross stood was traditionally identified as *gehinnom*, the Valley of Hinnom, from which we get *gehenna*. This is an English translation of the Greek *genna* and *gehannam* in the Quran in respective religious traditions.[102] This word came to mean a dark place, an abode for the punishment of those condemned to purgatory, and hell itself.[103] In Roman times, trees were kept burning there perpetually to incinerate the rubbish and filth that had been dumped, polluting the area with thick, black smoke and a pestilential stench. The biblical *gehenna* would have been an apt analogy for The Clarences as a dumping ground for other people's rubbish.

With fewer than twenty streets, The Clarences still struggles to shake off its negative image and to cope with high levels of unemployment, enduring poverty, unacceptable living conditions, and the many injustices visited on a socially-excluded community. Nearly every press report begins by describing the estate as "a deprived community", followed by "isolated" or "remote". Out of mind and out of sight, it has indeed become a dumping ground for waste of every description. However, even though the odds remain stacked against it, the community has been motivated to fight back in resisting further iniquities and to come together to create new ventures that promise a better future (see Chapters 11 and 12).

Absentee landlords are cited as one of the main problems, renovations and refurbishment not featuring on their agendas. Many houses are boarded up, the properties eventually being sold instead of being repaired and properly maintained. Neighbours are confronted daily by the depressing sight of empty, derelict buildings falling into ruin and gardens choked by weeds. As one resident, a retired soldier, was quoted as saying: "The problem here isn't the people. It's the people who are not here, the landlords." The estate's distance from nearby towns and the poor communication between them does not help, while anti-social behaviour among the young continues to be an issue, as well as a high crime rate, arson, and drug and alcohol abuse.[104]

In 2012, what was billed as Britain's cheapest house was on the market in Port Clarence for the starting price of £750. The three-bedroom property in Limetrees Close was boarded up and surrounded by a wilderness of weeds. The close itself was named "the cheapest street in Britain" and was particularly vulnerable to fly-tipping and arson. The house was actually sold at auction for £8,500. At the time, a property nearby was on the market for £1,000.[105]

Unfortunately, the underlying stigma of the place has endured. The estate is still said to be better known for its problems than for the people living there. An anonymous report published by iLiveHere in 2015 labelled Port Clarence "the worst place to live in England".[106] The statistics, largely compiled from the 2011 UK census figures, were presented according to a range of socio-economic factors, all negative with regard to the national average. These included education, unemployment and benefit rates, age distribution, the property market and rentals, and general health.

The report claimed that there were a high number of residents either with no qualifications or very low ones, that very few people were in any sort of meaningful employment, and that it was a place for the elderly with a poor health record. The rate of those claiming benefits, including work benefits, was said to be more than 25 per cent higher than the national average. It concluded that Port Clarence was an economically deprived area and that it would be hard to get a job if living there. Another recent report notes that unemployment in the Middlesbrough area, including The Clarences, is twice the national average, while child poverty is the third highest in the country. The statistics may vary slightly, but they all contain the same message.

Ironically, in 2015, the borough of Stockton-on-Tees, which includes The Clarences and their prosperous neighbouring town of Billingham, was billed as the fifth best place to live in the UK. This was according to new research published by *The Telegraph* and Hamptons International. The research ranks areas by a combination of affordability and residents' happiness, and is based on official data of house-price-to-income ratios and the Life Satisfaction Index.[107] This just goes to show how statistics can be manipulated to disguise the reality of poor, hidden communities.

During the period 2011 to 2013, the Church Action on Poverty North East group focused its attention on raising awareness among churches across the region of the all-pervading poverty in Britain.[108] It mounted a "Close the Gap" campaign supported by workshops. In 2013, a week-long campaign in St Nicholas' Cathedral, Newcastle, took "Breaking Barriers" as its theme. A theological reflection on exclusion noted that, in biblical stories, whatever could not be tolerated was put outside the camp or the city, rubbished. In like manner, there were many people in Britain who were rubbished, excluded from what might be regarded as normal participation in society.

Jesus, on the other hand, went about breaking down barriers—but at a price in sacrificing his life. The price had to be paid if barriers were to be smashed. The CAP report noted examples: physical ones as in Israel and Palestine; economic ones such as those which isolated Britain's under-class; and the impact caused by the disparity of income between rich and poor, the poor often being blamed by politicians and the super-rich for their poverty. The gap between the richest and the poorest in our society was said to be greater than at any other time in the last forty years, and yet poverty was so often kept out of sight as if it did not exist. CAP's aim was to encourage communities to take the lead in securing a greater share of a city council's budget.

The Clarences would surely exemplify the plight of an excluded people on all counts, and isolation has remained an ever-present reality. But the community has already taken a lead in forcing Stockton Borough Council to take notice of its needs and address them. The CAP campaign singled out the barriers to employment experienced by young people.

Like other young people on disadvantaged estates in the region, those in The Clarences were also discriminated against at the Job Centre. They were often pushed aside, rudely spoken to, and even threatened with police action. Regular reports of convictions at Teesside Magistrates' Court have not helped. These have included assaults by local youths on elderly people, burglaries, the petrol-bombing of a house, and drug possession and supply. But some young people are now receiving tertiary education and will be assured of a better life even if they have to find work elsewhere.

Arson is another perennial problem on the estate. In March 2011, a serious fire in the timber recycling plant burnt for nine days. The smoke was so thick that residents were advised to stay indoors and keep their windows closed. A couple of youngsters were taken into police custody, but not charged. Fly-tipping continues to be a contentious issue too. Other people's trash, like old mattresses, tyres, and refrigerators, are continually jettisoned from vehicles along the road. Garbage is also dumped in front of people's houses, outside their gardens where children play, and in the neighbouring fields.

This negative publicity must be extremely discouraging to those who have worked so hard to achieve transformation in the community and to lead honourable lives. What really hit the headlines, though, was the flooding of the estate in 2013 through no fault of the people themselves.

Early in December, a tidal surge combined with high spring tides broke through the flood defences along the Tees. It was the worst to hit the area in the 170 years of harbour master records. About three hundred homes and thirty-two businesses had to be evacuated, people being given temporary refuge in a leisure centre. At least half the houses suffered severe damage, the filthy river water leaving them full of sludge. Disinfectant had to be used in the clean-up operations. Days later, people were still living on the second floor of their homes. Many lost their most treasured possessions, such as family photographs. Although local businesses were badly hit as goods worth millions of pounds were washed away, they still helped by making pumps available to drain the flood water away. But the drying-out process and restoration of the properties was a long-term project.

The recovery from the devastation was eased by the strength of the community, the residents being widely praised for their resilience and fortitude. There was a real sense of camaraderie as they joined forces in offering each other aid. Young people were actively involved in helping to clear damaged households of goods and furniture. The Red Cross and the Billingham Legacy Foundation (BLF) were among those who provided active assistance. The BLF is a non-profit organization run by volunteers to support good causes in the surrounding area with funds and practical help.[109] Neighbouring churches and communities also came to the rescue and donations poured in. The High Clarence Primary School was used as a drop-in centre, money and goods being given to those most in need.

Necessary repairs were made, but water remained under the floorboards of some houses. The residents had to endure damp mould giving off an unpleasant, musty smell. It had been a terrifying experience and more than a year later the locals still lived in fear of further flooding ruining their homes and businesses yet again. At last, in May 2015, the Environment Agency began work on an extensive flood defence scheme along the Tees, which would give The Clarences greater protection. The estimated cost was £19 million.

The Tees Transporter Bridge, which dominates the Middlesbrough and Clarences skyline, celebrated its centenary in October 2011. However, it was closed to traffic in August 2013 for major refurbishment and to allow for the flood defence work to proceed. This included raising the approach road to the Transporter. Unexpected repairs to the bridge sent the cost of the renovations spiralling to £4 million, of which the Heritage Lottery Fund (HLF) contributed £2.6 million. The bridge opened briefly during 2014 before being closed again for further work. More delays were caused by a sub-contractor entering administration.

The Transporter was finally reopened to the public on 9 March 2015. Passage was free for the first few weeks to offset the inconvenience of the delays. The gondola now has a newly installed glass viewing lift offering panoramic views of the Tees. The visitor centre has also been refurbished with new interpretation displays.[110] But, for The Clarences' community, the long closure of the bridge meant that it was more isolated than ever. However, it was the discovery that it really was being used as a dumping ground for non-hazardous and hazardous waste that was the last straw.

Once this became public, opposition was mounted with furious publicity and petitions.

Augean Oil and Gas had initially specialized in treating waste materials from oil and gas sites in the North Sea. Subsequently, Augean Treatment Limited, licensed by the Environment Agency, used landfills on derelict brownfield sites in the former industrial area alongside The Clarences. It pumped in a mixture of hazardous toxic waste, such as asbestos, oil, and material from chemical manufacturing, and non-hazardous household rubbish.

In 2014, a European ruling required that hazardous waste must be placed in separate sites. Augean maintains that all its waste which is destined for landfill, both hazardous and non-hazardous, is pre-treated according to clearly defined regulations.[111] It is also said to follow strict rules about what can be disposed of in hazardous landfills. These include contaminated soils, asbestos, stabilized waste, and residues from recovery operations. It was hoping to extend its contract after it ran out in 2016 so that its landfill sites could be filled to capacity.[112] But nothing was said about radioactive radium waste. It was only in May 2013 that Port Clarence residents discovered that the government had secretly dumped this material right on their doorstep.

The residents were horrified to learn that, nearly fifty years after the Cold War, much of this highly toxic material had been buried in nearby landfill sites without their knowledge. The waste was from controversial nuclear bomb tests carried out on Christmas Island in the South Pacific at the height of the Cold War in 1958. Ex-servicemen who witnessed the tests have spoken out against this shocking discovery. At the time secrecy prevailed, but they believe that the lives of many of them have been ruined by the after-effects of exposure to the fallout, and that their children have suffered birth defects as a result. The veterans claim that they were not properly protected during the trials and were just told to cover their eyes when the blasts took place. They have long been campaigning for compensation. Native islanders were not evacuated during the tests and also claim to have suffered from exposure to radiation.[113]

In 2008, up to thirty tonnes of radioactive sand that was left over on the island was secretly transported back to the UK and deposited at the Port Clarence landfill site together with tonnes of lead and asbestos. This was hushed up by the Ministry of Defence (MoD). A Clarence veteran commented: "They say that this stuff in the landfill is very low-level radiation waste, but if that is the case why have they transported it more than eight thousand miles across the world to dump it in Port Clarence?" Another local veteran, who was stationed with the Royal Navy during the nuclear tests and has suffered serious health problems since, said: "I thought I had left that behind—it's like it has followed me home after all these years."[114]

The Environment Agency, the MoD, and the Augean operators contend that the nuclear waste only contains low levels of radiation. According to their spokesman, the waste poses no danger to members of the public and the site is fully equipped to operate with hazardous waste. But angry residents in Port Clarence believe they should have been warned, and called for an enquiry.

Simon Burnett, who lives at Limetrees Close, was quoted as saying: "For people like me who have kids, this is really worrying. It's right next to where we live. No one ever told us about this kind of radioactive waste being dumped. It's shocking. Our government is supposed to look after us, but they agreed to move this stuff halfway round the world, only to dump it near our house." Jean Bradley, who lives nearest to the site at Saltview Terrace, said: "I've lived here for twenty years. I knew they had dumped dead cows after the foot-and-mouth disease, but not this. I'm shocked."[115] A survey showed that the land was found to have "slightly elevated levels of radioactivity". But this was little comfort to the local community.

On our visit in 2015, the whole matter seemed to have died down. We were assured that high-level nuclear waste produced by the power station at Hartlepool was stored on-site and was not seen to pose any threat to the surrounding area.

Contemplative Meditation of Hildegard of Bingen (1098–1179)

I heard a voice speaking against the crimes
which members of religious communities
as well as lay people commit against justice:
"O justice, you are without a homeland;
you are a foreigner in the city . . .
'Whence do I come?
I come from the heart of the Father . . .
I sigh at the ignorance of the people.'"

Taken from a letter to an abbot, quoted in
Illuminations of Hildegard of Bingen[116]

CHAPTER 11

Servant Leadership at Work

Above all, preserve an intense love for each other, since love covers over many a sin. Welcome each other into your houses without grumbling. Each one of you has received a special grace, so, like good stewards responsible for all these varied graces of God, put it at the service of others. If anyone is a speaker, let it be as the words of God, if any one serves, let it be in strength granted by God.

1 Peter 4. 8–11

It is over a decade since Imelda and Philippa left The Clarences, so in the autumn of 2015 I was accompanied by Fr Jayant Kothare while visiting the estate. We had little idea of what to expect, except what we had gleaned from press reports and the internet. Crossing the Tees from Middlesbrough via the refurbished Transporter Bridge, with its glass-walled gondola, was a promising start, as were the impressive flood defences on the river banks. This was followed by a few disappointments, but even more encouraging discoveries.

Where the Sisters left off, members of the community have picked up the task of nurturing mission from below. They have continued to do their own theological thinking on everyday issues which concern them. Their theology from below has facilitated many more positive initiatives. The values which the Sisters implanted by their example and their work in creating a Kingdom community were deeply rooted. In the interim, however, the problems with which the estate has had to contend seem to have grown worse. Despite this, the community is making a laudable attempt to hold these values together. The people have directed their energies in creative ways that are a reflection of the culture in which they live.

The single-minded dedication and spirituality of the Sisters cannot be replaced. Instead, as is typical of mission from below, a new form of servant leadership has emerged involving a number of people in a variety of ways. Working as a team, they combine forces in tackling the most pressing issues. Even though the Sisters are sorely missed, they have left behind a rich legacy in terms of an ethic of team spirit, mission from below, grass-roots theology, environmental healing, women's leadership, a secular spirituality, and, last but not least, a militant faith in people power. This legacy has ensured that the model of servant leadership is zealously followed in The Clarences.

Naturally, there are a few disappointments. The Hub has a rather run-down and deserted appearance. The café closed after the lease expired and there have been no new offers. The Citizens Advice Bureau in the community centre has also closed. There is no community nurse in the health centre, although the part-time post has been advertised, and a doctor only comes for a few hours a week. The Co-op, however, is busy and, judging by the noise, the crèche is alive and well. A recent report by a housing association claims that this small village maintains "a high community spirit".[117] This was confirmed by the people we met.

We were fortunate that, at the start of our visit, the Clarences' Residents' Action Group (CRAG) was holding its monthly meeting. It maintains regular contact with Stockton Borough Council, Tristar Homes, and Cleveland Police. In June 2012, a Neighbourhood Agreement was entered into to address eleven priorities for the estate, including health, safety, and transport. A scrutiny panel has been deputed to meet regularly to discuss progress, holding those accountable to address outstanding issues. Security, for one, has vastly improved with CCTV coverage of many properties.[118] The Peace Centre now seems to be used for business meetings, with a large table and chairs filling the room.

CRAG has formed partnerships with local agencies such as those that provided funding and helped with the clean-up operations after the flood. For example, the Billingham Environmental Link Programme (BELP) made improvements to the allotments and green areas. After the CRAG meeting, Kevin Pitt, a retired senior police officer from Billingham, gave us a conducted tour of the huge community garden which he has created (see Chapter 12). Funding is a constant headache and the Billingham Legacy Foundation (BLF) continues to provide active support for social functions and events. Here, the moving spirit is Pat Chambers, editor of the *Billingham Community Newspaper* (*BCN*). Both she and Kevin confessed that they were inspired by the Sisters' example to offer their services to The Clarences.

"Christmas in The Clarences" began when a woman complained to Pat that "Christmas doesn't come here anymore". So they devised a wish list—a selection box for each child, reindeer dust food (a porridge and glitter mix), and decorations in the community centre. They met with more members of the community so that all would be involved in making Christmas a special time in Port Clarence.[119] Pat secured a selection box for each child and bought the required ingredients. The residents' group then put together 150 reindeer food bags for the children. This time together inspired more ideas of what they could do and decorations were made to dress up the centre.

Pat then went about obtaining funds to buy the children "good presents". She also secured help from her Billingham community—a baker offered to provide mince pies, the Northfield School orchestra was invited to play music, and Churches Together (of which The Clarences are a part) promised to lead the singing of carols. Candy floss and popcorn machines were lent. McDonalds donated tea, coffee, and juice, and Asda (Walmart) supplied decorations to make a Santa's grotto in the meeting room (the former Peace Centre). The Wilton Engineering Group in The Clarences even agreed to make Santa a sleigh. All that remained on the wish list was a Christmas tree, but this was proving a more difficult ask as time was so short.

Then, just before Christmas 2013, came the unprecedented freak weather conditions when an exceptionally high tide was accompanied by driving rain and gale-force winds. As the storm surge forced high waves into the Tees estuary, the river broke its banks. Wilton Engineering was directly in the path of the floodwater and the firm lost millions of pounds worth of goods. But the handsome sleigh became iconic in that it stayed firm on its plinths as the turbulence raged around it. The owner said that many of his men cried because, in the midst of such devastation, the sleigh was still "good to go".

The party went ahead too, although the rooms had been filled with water. An anxious child asked whether Santa would still come. But, as Pat says: "A host of angels descended and helped clean and dry the rooms." They cleared Santa's grotto of its layers of mud and sludge, put up the decorations and "filled the room with lots of Christmas magic". Residents baked mince pies and gingerbread, and prepared a feast for all. About one hundred and fifty children received gifts, and there was music, carols, a pantomime, games, and much festive cheer. One little boy almost suffocated Santa when he hugged him tightly, saying: "I knew you would still come." Since then, Christmas parties have become an annual community event.

After the Sisters left, the baton was picked up by CRAG as best it could. Apart from trying to continue some social ministry, it has aimed to take a leading role in cementing the community together and to bring joy into people's lives. It organizes fun events and outings such as Christmas shopping for those who would otherwise never leave the estate. Its annual family fun day is run in partnership with the Thirteen Housing Group, with the support of local sponsors. In 2015, a jam-packed day included a bouncy castle, balloon modelling, a giant inflatable, a magic show, a variety of craft and gardening stalls, and food and drinks. Fire engines brought by the Cleveland Fire Brigade were a star attraction, with the children being allowed to climb on board and chat to the officers.[120] These events resonate with the local culture and provide some excitement in what can be a rather drab existence.[121]

The Families Group meets once a week. Its aim is to build strong and sustainable families through mutual support. It organizes talks on subjects such as weight loss, healthy eating, and giving up smoking. At other times, members might make crafts, bake bread, or cook nutritious soups. They had a strategic role following the flood. As one member said: "It is in our interest to have a community that can look after itself and is proud of itself."

We were told that changes in government funding have been disastrous. Politically, the government wants a community to take more initiative in delivery through local strategic partnerships. No wonder that fundraising is high on the CRAG agenda. In January 2015, it took part for the first time in the *Evening Gazette* Wish Windfall campaign. Participants had to collect as many tokens as possible from the daily newspaper, money being apportioned according to the number of tokens collected. In the CRAG application, secretary Leanne McCabe said: "I grew up here and know what the area is like. We wish to get more funding to do more activities." Even the local schoolchildren were roped in to collect tokens.

The local press has played a significant role in keeping The Clarences in the limelight. Pat Chambers, editor of the *BCN*, always includes news of their doings.[122] Special events are celebrated with pages of colourful photographs. The free paper, founded in 2010, comes out every six weeks. Twenty thousand copies are delivered to all letter boxes in Billingham and the surrounding villages. Communication is vital in getting people involved in all that is happening.

The paper is run by a handful of volunteers, who aim "to turn the tide of a sea of negatives and bad news to deliver a publication filled cover to cover with positives about good people achieving great things, helping to raise aspirations in young and old alike, and contributing towards community cohesion". It uses a quote from Dr Seuss in its heading: "Unless someone like you cares a whole awful lot, nothing is going to get better. It's not."[123]

High Clarence Primary School was last on our visit. With its dedicated teachers, it has maintained an exceptional record, providing special facilities for its many pupils who come from disadvantaged homes. The headteacher, Jean Orridge OBE, welcomed us with a small group of pupils. We were presented with large cards decorated with a collage of pictures drawn by the children. Our small hosts then took us on a guided tour of the school, visiting every classroom. Surrounded by colourful works of art and learning aids, the pupils were happily absorbed in their work. They include a number of Roma children, whose families have lived locally for generations. Once the recent Polish intake learnt English, they excelled. Some families have moved away because of transport difficulties, but newcomers have been attracted by the cheap housing. Taking into account all the educational challenges, Ofsted reports continue to be outstanding.

We then met with Jean Orridge and her vice-principal over lunch. When Imelda's post as family liaison officer ended, she continued working with the families, especially at the weekends. She was a vital link in finding out what was happening on the ground. Trained in child guidance and educational psychology, Philippa was also closely involved with families. Having earned the children's trust, she was invaluable in providing a listening ear and in helping to sort out their problems. With the Sisters' wide educational experience, they believed that children can only be receptive to schooling if they, their families, and their social environment are healthy.

After the Sisters left, people in distress had nowhere to go, so the school became their port of call. They come almost every day looking for help, whether about evictions, health matters, family disputes, crime, or drug and alcohol abuse. Jean does what she can to assist and visits the children's homes. The teachers help in identifying problems and give support where it is acceptable. For Jean, The Clarences could almost be described as an inner-city village: "The children have such a hard journey to go down because of no early training. More have to be given school meals than before as well." Imelda and Philippa had a "Poverty Churches Pot", which they gave Jean.

A speech and language unit now visits weekly. This is a boon as previously pupils had to go to Stockton and would be struck off the list if they failed to attend. Many come from disadvantaged homes, and improved literacy gives them greater confidence. With no church on the estate, the children know little about religion. Janet Capstick, a Methodist minister, visits regularly to assist and does some counselling. Clergy also visit occasionally and hold services in the new school hall.

At one stage Churches Together in Billingham set up a foodbank in the Hub. Initially, families were reluctant to come forward, but this is now a weekly service without which many of them simply would not eat. This was vital during Christmas 2015. The churches have also suffered cuts and their workload doubled. Anglican Church members have now been incorporated within the newly established Billingham Team Ministry in the Stockton Deanery of the Diocese of Durham.[124] Three Roman Catholic parishes were brought together under the title of St Thomas of Canterbury, the former patron saint of the mother parish of Port

Clarence. But there are still no church buildings to provide a focal point on the estate. Indeed, the churches have been physically absent for so long that at present true transformation is taking place in the community.

Our final meeting was with members of CRAG over tea at the school. Health and transport problems are their main worries. The school nurse treats the children, but otherwise they have to go to Billingham. Although the town is only three miles down the road, beyond the remains of Haverton, it is an eight-mile bus ride via Middlesbrough. They would rather save the money for food. The long closure of the Transporter had not helped. The council's bus subsidy was also withdrawn two years ago as the bus was not thought to be economically viable. People walk to Billingham to buy food as it is cheaper in the supermarkets than in local shops. Some get online deliveries, but they still have to pay delivery charges.

At night, young people will walk to Billingham and back just to get out and have some fun. The nearest bank is also there, so there is a move afoot to start a credit union. The lack of transport is a real burden and the women feel the isolation. "The nuns would have been our voice for health and transport," they said. "It needs someone with time, willingness, and energy to tackle the problem."

Fuel poverty remains an issue. It is hoped that Community Switch will be effective in organizing lower tariffs, as promised. Pollution is still a problem too. Small trucks pass through with smelly waste, while the heavy trucks thunder past the school, the drivers often hurling verbal abuse. The lack of recreational facilities for the young has always been a problem. One resident said: "There is little for them to do. They have no aspirations, no dreams." Some voluntary work is done with the youngsters, but government cuts mean that there are no social services to deal with the crisis. There is an urgent need for organized activities like youth clubs, drama, music, field trips, and camping. To make matters worse, troublemakers are now sent to the estate together with their problem families.

A growing concern is the drop in numbers at the school as teachers might have to be withdrawn. Jean Orridge performs wonders in keeping them all together. If the school were to close, the place would disintegrate. Some of the women said they would move away as they could see no future without jobs. Despite all this, they all felt that there was still a strong sense of being a family community: "Everybody looks after everybody else. We stand together even when life is difficult and learn to live with all that is bad."

Since the Sisters left, women have followed their example in taking a leading role in holding the community together. Words like "bonding", "empowerment", "self-confidence", and "self-respect" came up regularly in our conversation. In the Church, they would have been relegated to subservient roles like cleaning and catering. Without a communal meeting place in the Hub, they enjoy chatting to each other in the doctor's waiting room, outside the school, or on their doorsteps. They remain surprisingly cheerful in the face of all their difficulties.

The women had many amusing stories about Imelda. "If she were here", said one, "we wouldn't have to go through all this. She knew how to make a fuss at getting money. Kicked them up their backsides. Those at the top just seem to protect themselves." They never see their councillors now, even though they are invited to meetings, and expect no help from them. "We are deprived of our rights", they said. "Imelda would have sorted them out. She would do anything for you. It was also impossible to say 'no' to her, religious or not. We all miss her so much."

The Clarences have always been a close-knit community. They just needed the Sisters to come alongside them to provide the necessary motivation and spiritual strength to triumph over the iniquities that bedevil their lives. As a case study of what it is like to be poor and powerless in modern-day Britain, at the mercy of every sort of injustice, this story of a courageous community provides an inspiring example of how mission from below, given the right sort of servant leadership, can move mountains. It provides a beacon of hope to many others in similar situations.

It must truly be considered a blessing in disguise that in their dire hour of need the residents of The Clarences were without the benefit of a Church presence. We did not witness any anti-clerical sentiment, yet we did not find any hankering for their own church either. It appears that the community is now in a phase where it would welcome Kingdom growth far more than Church growth.

The Story of Brother Lawrence (1614–1691)

Brother Lawrence, known for his writings on prayer, was a lay member of an abbey in Paris. He worked in the kitchen and repaired sandals. He died in obscurity. He wrote in his journal: "We can do little things for God. I turn the cake that is frying on the pan, for love of God. That done, if there is nothing else to call me, I prostrate myself in worship before the One who has given me grace to work."[125]

This practice of taking pride in little things for God is characteristically Celtic. The Celtic Church inspired the people to look for the extraordinary in the ordinary. Even the most prosaic, workaday chores are a sacramental offering to God.

The Greening of The Clarences

O Greenness of God's Finger
with which God built a vineyard,
You are glorious in God's preparation
for greening the earth.
Hildegard of Bingen (1098–1179)[126]

Hildegard von Bingen, who wrote this glorious invocation, talks about God's redemptive presence in terms of "greening" and compares Jesus to the finger of God. She coined the Latin word *viriditas*, which has been variously translated as healing, moisture, freshness, vitality, life-force, fecundity, etc. She views the greening as infusing creation not only spiritually, but also at every layer of matter, be it earth, trees, rivers, base metal, the flesh, and animals, down to the last atom. Hildegard claimed that this cosmic greening, which is an innate activity of God, heals, transforms, and redeems the world.

Hildegard is unique in expounding this green theology, possibly owing to the verdant lushness of her monastic surroundings in the village of Disibodenberg in her native Rhineland in Germany. She is the first theologian to identify ecological healing as an inalienable aspect of redemption in Christ. She has also made us realize that we would not truly honour God if we did not care for God's creation. Thanks to Hildegard, we now know that no justice is complete without environmental justice.

In recent times, St Francis has been acclaimed as the patron saint of ecology because of his affinity with the stars and the animals. But Hildegard's understanding of ecology is much more comprehensive than just what one may regard as nature mysticism. When she talks about the greening, it is not just about Mother Nature. For her, it is also the greening of our souls, our minds, our emotions, our thoughts, our aspirations, our hopes, our relationships, our communities, and all that makes us human. Her ecology embraces the whole gamut of creation, from biology to psychology and sociology.

In a place like The Clarences, or for that matter any other deprived area in the North of England, the concept of Hildegard's vision of ecology is a realistic blueprint by which entire communities could be sanitized, regenerated, developed, and enabled to prosper. Ecology from this broad viewpoint reaches much further than our usual understanding; it encompasses our parks, our roads, our gardens, our homes, our physical health, our mental well-being, our schools, our diet, community cohesion, job creation, youth counselling, care for the elderly, safety in public areas, domestic harmony, community-friendly public and private enterprises, a crime-free environment, clean and unpolluted air and water supply, sanctuaries for birds and animals, and much more. We invite our readers to add their personal concerns to this blessed list of what would constitute a total ecological greening of their respective communities as envisaged by Hildegard.

"Greening The Clarences" is probably one of the most challenging projects Kevin Pitt has tackled since he retired as a Chief Superintendent of Cleveland Police. After gaining a postgraduate degree in ecological psychology, he founded the Billingham Environmental Link Programme (BELP) in 2010, and is its director and strategic manager. From his headquarters at The Place in Billingham he has initiated numerous environmental projects to regenerate the surrounding area.

As a servant leader, he has the same commitment to working alongside people and empowering them to improve their lives as did Imelda and Philippa. Indeed, they have been an inspiration to him, more especially through their efforts in energizing the community, and their initial ecological vision in creating a Peace Garden. His dedication to ecological justice, and his mentoring and redirection of youngsters who have fallen foul of the law to better themselves, would also mesh with the Sisters' socio-economic concerns.[127]

BELP is a not-for-profit organization run by the community for the community, undertaking projects locally with a view to driving the physical, social, and economic regeneration of Billingham and neighbouring communities, including The Clarences. It aims to work with the people of Teesside in re-using redundant land which has become an eyesore, and creating pleasing environments which enhance the area. These projects are also designed to provide local employment for the benefit of the whole community. So far, it has developed a horticultural and agricultural project, and a rockery. Future plans include developing a wildlife garden and a wildlife corridor, and landscaping on a 1.3-mile-long railway embankment with the full support of owners Network Rail.[128]

BELP has a particular interest in motivating young ex-offenders to turn their lives around by recruiting them in projects while helping to transform industrial land into nature reserves. In 2013, when Kevin was nominated as a *Gazette* Community Champion, he was lauded for his work in bringing young and old together to collaborate with various organizations. He was especially commended for his ability to bring out the best in people and make them feel proud of their community. He had helped some of the most prolific offenders in Stockton to come off drugs, enter gainful employment, and go on to college.[129] In 2014, he won the Catalyst Outstanding Achievement Award for his community work. Of note was his passion within BELP for helping long-term unemployed people into full-time employment and providing social and financial support to families suffering most from the reforms in welfare. The award was given in recognition of his work in the voluntary and community sector.[130]

Following in the Loreto Sisters' footsteps, Kevin has been working alongside residents of The Clarences to develop a community garden. This was officially opened in December 2015 as part of the estate's Christmas celebrations. It is still a work in progress. At Port Clarence, a partnership was established between BELP and Groundwork North East and Cumbria. It has an environmental investment programme to improve the appearance of local neighbourhoods.[131]

Mission from below can take on many different forms and is forever open to exploring new directions, unhindered by those in power. In this instance, the environment has become the backdrop on which The Clarences community has been given the opportunity to transform part of the post-industrial wasteland on its borders into a Garden of Eden. Everyone has been recruited in this new venture. Young and old, male and female, the able and the disabled, the poor and those better off, believers and non-believers, war veterans and ex-criminal offenders, all have been brought together to renew the earth and establish facilities for relaxation, recreation, and training. Neither is there any shortage of ideas as to how to extend the range of activities.

Around the world, community gardens provide fresh produce, more neighbourliness across the board, a sense of community, and a heightened respect and concern for enhancing the environment. Health is improved through increased vegetable and fruit consumption, and regular physical exercise. The Westlowthian Street Community Garden at Port Clarence provides all these positive outcomes and more. One of Kevin's greatest challenges was to overcome an endemic project fatigue and disillusionment engendered by the many short-term efforts begun by social organizations which were then terminated with minimal results. He had so to engage the community that the project would be seen to belong to it and that it would be responsible for its continuation in the long term.

Working alongside and not lording it over people, affording them full freedom to conceive a task, initiating a project but not then taking over, listening to their concerns, accepting one's own limitations in leadership and owning up to one's mistakes and shortcomings, adopting a ministry of presence without seeming to be meddling, taking no credit for success but giving due recognition to others for their contribution, no matter how small—in short, leading without leading is the secret of servant leadership.

Figure 13: The Wasteland Before Clearing (Pat Chambers)

Figure 14: The Original Condition of the Site (Kevin Pitt)

The Westlowthian Street allotment land being used for the garden at Port Clarence is on contract from the Council and was chosen as being the worst piece of ground on the estate. Photographs show huge truckloads of asbestos and rubbish left by fly-tipping having to be removed before any work could begin. The place is now surrounded by a high fence with locked gates as a safety precaution to prevent vandalism.

The property has been divided up into a horticultural centre with large polytunnels, the community garden, and small allotments with a training area.[132] So far, more than one hundred people from the community have availed themselves of these facilities. A variety of flowers and seasonal vegetables are grown in large raised boxes, neatly set out with paths in between. The gardeners take enough for their own use and then give away the rest. Boxes of vegetables are left on the doorsteps of those in need on the estate.

Figure 15: The Community Garden (Pat Chambers)

**Figure 16: A Resident with her Grandson in the
Adults' and Children's Garden (Kevin Pitt)**

Local statistics show that obesity, especially among children and teenagers, is on the rise, with more than twenty per cent of a household's income being spent on food. In Billingham alone there are twenty-one takeaway outlets purveying junk food in a two-mile area. Both children and their parents require education on healthy eating, all of which the garden hopes to provide.

The community garden is parcelled into four quadrants. An area has been set aside for the interdenominational Churches Together in Billingham and the surrounding area. It is represented by thirteen churches, including Roman Catholics, Anglicans, Methodists, Baptists, and other faith communities. This garden was ready by March 2016. A minister comes once a month and is available for counselling for a few hours in the Faith Garden. The local Methodist church raised the funds to erect a cabin in one corner. Volunteers from two local firms, Augean Waste Management and Avecia, created a beautiful pond backed by a rockery, together with a patio area. There were also plans to install a statue of St Francis of Assisi close by.

Figure 17: Faith Cabin available to Site Users (Kevin Pitt)

Adjoining them is the adults' and children's garden, and they are actively involved in developing their land. Grandmothers can be seen hard at work with their grandchildren. A community orchard has been planted in one corner too, with a selection of fruit trees. A third section has been set aside for those who are mentally challenged and physically disabled. The final area was being developed for the Royal British Legion and over-60s and was finished in 2016.

In the centre of the garden is the Baltic labyrinth made of bricks. Unlike most labyrinths, it is square and has an entrance and an exit. Apart from its purpose for meditation, the space is used for social activities and musical performances. A large cabin sited nearby is available for social and church events, Christmas trading, therapeutic work for mental health, and drug and alcohol recovery programmes. The Sisters' work in regenerating and expanding the Hub as a community centre has now found a new home, so realizing their ongoing vision. Two projects in the pipeline are beekeeping for children and a chicken farm. There are also plans for a compost area and worm farm.

There is a continual need for funding and organizers are kept busy making bids to likely sponsors. BLF, for one, has been very supportive. This charitable group encourages people in the community to invest money in ethical issues and to benefit the locals. For example, it provided a man with a bus season ticket to get to his work in Sunderland. Previously, in order to keep his job, he had to walk those many miles as he did not have the bus fare. Wilton Engineering, opposite the centre, also promised to lend a crane to move the large cabin across the garden. This would have been a very expensive operation without aid.

With the government cuts in training, the problem has arisen as to how young people can be educated to enter the job market. The purpose of the Care in the Community Programme run by BELP at the garden is to teach youths aged eleven to seventeen, who have become socially isolated, skills in gardening as well as other skills and activities. This would enable them to become qualified and self-employed, or else sponsored as apprentices. Horticultural training would provide qualifications at Levels 1 and 2.

Billingham has the largest ageing population in the Stockton area. There is, therefore, a need for the gardens of private homes in the community to be kept clean and tidy at a reasonable remuneration. Not only would the young people learn new skills, but being in work would build up their self-worth and work discipline while helping older residents, in particular. The residents would also like to start a music club. The young people would learn to play various instruments, providing them with another source of income as well as a pleasurable occupation. The lessons would be free. Recreational and sports facilities are another priority.[133]

Volunteers from home and abroad have also caught the vision of this community project and are eager to do their bit. School-leavers from in and around Billingham chose the community gardens in Port Clarence as part of their hands-on training through the National Careers Service (NCS). The idea was that those who were not proceeding into higher education would be able to explore a practical route to a possible apprenticeship. The young people spent two weeks in the gardens clearing weeds, levelling ground, helping to build a rockery, and planting flowers and seeds. They did a great job and were praised for their help.[134]

In July 2014, eleven members from Burnt Hickory Baptist Church in Atlanta, Georgia, worked for five days in developing the Churches Together section of the garden. Their task was to build a Faith Wall. They were part of a group of 115 young people who, with their mentors, were in the North East on a service mission called Radiate. The selection process required that the volunteers had to be members of a church choir. After their morning's work was done, they then went on to sing in local churches.[135]

Some of the Augean employees live in Port Clarence. Amazed at seeing the allotments transformed from a dumping ground filled with rubbish and contaminated waste into a flourishing garden, they too wanted to give something back to the local community. With the full support of their station manager, a group of volunteers stopped operating their mobile plant and got to work with spades and wheelbarrows. They removed barrow-loads of soil and rocks to make two ponds and to finish off building the rockery.[136]

Planting trees, clearing land, wiping out pollution, cleaning our ponds, rivers and seas, adopting a sustainable and simple lifestyle, conserving non-renewable natural resources, protecting members of the animal kingdom, and all else that is called for in our campaign to heal our ecosystem, form only one part of being stewards of God's creation. One must take into consideration the cosmic fact that all imbalance in the ecosphere comes from our skewed relationship with God. Ecological devastation is linked with our lack of spiritual and ethical integrity. Unless we repair our relationship with God we cannot heal Mother Earth. In God's court, we stand accused before the desecrated creation.

The Old Testament prophet Micah challenges the human race:

> Now listen to what Yahweh says:
> "Stand up, state your case to the mountains
> and let the hills hear what you have to say!"
> Listen, mountains, to the case as Yahweh puts it, give ear,
> you foundations of the earth,
> for Yahweh has a case against his people
> and he will argue it with Israel.
>
> *Micah 6. 1-2*

Ecology is not a secular, New Age agenda, but very much part of God's mission. It is not we, but God, who shall renew, heal, and redeem the earth desecrated by us. Ultimately, we are only servants of God's ministry and praying participants in his greening mission:

> I shall turn the desert into a lake and dry ground into springs of water. I shall plant the desert with cedar trees, acacias, myrtles and olives; in the wastelands I shall put cypress trees, plane trees and box trees side by side; so that people may see and know, so that they may all observe and understand that the hand of Yahweh has done this, that the Holy One of Israel has created it.
>
> *Isaiah 41. 18–20*

Hymn by Hildegard of Bingen

> O Fire of the Holy Spirit,
> life of the life of every creature,
> holy are you in giving life to forms.
> O boldest path
> penetrating into all places,
> in the heights, on earth,
> and in every abyss,
> you bring and bind all together.
> From you clouds flow, air flies,
> rocks have their humours,
> rivers spring forth from the waters,
> and the Earth is clothed
> with your Greening breath.
>
> *From the hymn "O ignis Spiritus Paracliti"*

Epilogue

Amidst the doom and gloom over the decline of the Church in England, our story strikes a note of hope and expectancy. Traditionally, mission encompasses evangelism and pastoral care. The former, through conversion, promotes Church growth. The latter, involving ambulance ministry, serves people's immediate needs. The deeper socio-economic and political issues facing a community remain unchallenged and unchanged. But the story of the Loreto Sisters' mission in The Clarences, on the River Tees, bridges the personal and the political, contemplation and social transformation, the healing of body and mind as well as the environment.

Their mission was not about growing the Church, but rather, about growing a community in terms of a better quality of life for all regardless of creed, ethnicity, gender, age, and class. Supported throughout by prayer, it was about empowering the residents of a deprived estate in the North East, a forgotten people in a forgotten place, to fight for their liberation and for justice. This mission was not conducted by the Church from above, but by the people themselves from below.

Starting with a listening presence, and emulating the self-effacing ministry of Jesus and the saints, the Sisters set an example of servant leadership. This meant that instead of leading from the front, as was the customary way of doing mission, they came alongside the people, giving them the confidence to take matters into their own hands to bring about radical change. That this model of mission took birth, and has not only survived but grown in new directions in what has been designated as the worst place to live in England, is a miracle. It is a sure sign of hope that the Christian mission has been restored to its kenotic, egalitarian roots in the land of Aidan, Cuthbert, Hilda, and Bede. In mission from below the community takes the responsibility for its own spiritual nurture, honouring its saintly forebears and the folk spirituality that they spawned.

The idea of mission as community growth is germane to the debate. When the Baptist sent his men to Jesus with the query: "Are you the One to come?", he is wanting to be assured that Jesus was indeed the long-awaited leader. But Jesus does not give him a direct answer. Instead, he says: "Go and tell John what you hear and see; the blind receive their sight and the lame walk, lepers are cleansed and the deaf hear, the dead are raised up, and the poor have good news preached to them." (Matthew 11. 1–5). Jesus was not interested in asserting his identity as a Messianic leader, but was explaining how the community around him was growing thanks to his servant leadership.

In an increasingly pluralistic world, the language of the Kingdom is the new discourse of faith, which has come to define mission. As the Church declines and the pews remain empty, we are wont to blame the multitude of religious and secular ideologies with which we now have to compete. However, Jesus is arguably the most revered and acclaimed icon in world history. Even agnostics and atheists usually have a grudging word of acknowledgement for him. This is the same Jesus whom Christians proclaim and believe in. Why then does our evangelism meet with unbelief from the rest of the world?

The Jesus who commands humanity's respect is identified with social justice, sacrificial love, and compassion for the poor. He is the emblem of selfless service promoting healing, peace, and reconciliation. In our theological jargon, we call him Son of God, the Messiah, the Saviour, and the like. These terms fail to resonate in our wounded world desperately looking for Kingdom values, which would bring about a real change in our everyday lives. We need to learn to speak, think, and act in Kingdom terms.

The dilemma with traditional mission is that it offers the person of Jesus but not his Kingdom. We strive for Church growth rather than the nurturing of our ravaged communities. There is a plethora of books dreaming up ever new fresh expressions of church designed to fill our pews and save our dying churches. We hold up as an ideal Jesus' self-giving on the cross, yet we have built church structures which are locked into a straitjacket of power and hierarchical authority. We preach equality of all in Christ while at the same time ordinary folk are too often disempowered. They are there to pray, pay, and obey. When Gandhi was once asked about his views on Christianity, he replied: "Yes, it is a lovely idea." Unless we acknowledge the radical transformation of our communities as the incarnational basis of our Christian mission, the institutional Church will continue to decline.

In the Sisters' mission in The Clarences, preaching was not a feature. It was their exemplary life of prayer and their care of the community that said it all. Through their listening presence and active involvement behind the scenes, they touched people's hearts and minds more than any words from a pulpit would have done. Those who were previously ignorant or uninterested in the gospel now came on board. St Francis is reputed to have exhorted his followers to go out into the world and preach the gospel at all times, and only if necessary to use words. This was the model suited to the mission from below.

The Eucharist is the sacrament and covenant that defines our collective Christian journey. It embodies the healing, transformation, and redemption of our fallen world through Jesus' self-giving. The account of the Last Supper is narrated in three of the four Gospels. We find it in Matthew 26. 26–29, Mark 14. 22–25, Luke 22. 14–20, and 1 Corinthians 11. 23–26. The one conspicuous detail the three Gospels share is that they unequivocally link the sacrament with the Kingdom and not with the Church: "I tell you I shall not drink again of this fruit of the vine until that day when I drink it with you in my Father's kingdom." (Matthew and Mark); "I shall not eat it until it is fulfilled in the Kingdom of God." (Luke). Luke even refers to the Kingdom twice in the space of two verses.

When Jesus breaks bread, his invitation is open to all those who are hungry for justice and wholeness. The eleven who sat around him at the table represented the common folk who did not seek any membership of any religious group but simply to belong to the Kingdom where, in Christ, they could become truly and fully human. The Holy Communion is not a private but a collective sacrament. It is the new covenant of the Kingdom itself, which is open to all. It is sad that we Christians identify the sacrament with being members of the Church and not with being active servants in the mission to heal and transform the world, which God so loved and for which Jesus gave up his life. How often do we reflect on the Kingdom when we receive the sacrament at our church altar rails?

True mission belongs to the Holy Spirit. The Sisters had no specific goals when they started work in what was then a ghost town, but left everything to the Spirit to guide them in their ministry. This is the hallmark of authentic servant leadership. Out of the uncertainty emerged a mission which let people develop on their own terms and at their own pace. The Sisters did not manipulate or manage anything or anyone. There were no imperatives or restrictions. All they had to offer was their enduring encouragement. If the path ahead was dark, they were content to take one step at a time. When assailed by doubts, they sought guidance in prayer. As far as the day-to-day ministry went, their only framework was the Kingdom of Jesus, which embraces one and all regardless of who you are.

After sixteen years of unstinting service, they left as quietly as they had come. But their legacy lives on. The baton was passed to the women who form the Residents' Action Group and the Families Group, the editor of the community newspaper, the headteacher of the primary school, and a retired senior police officer who has inspired the flourishing community garden. There are also the many unsung servants who have nurtured mission in The Clarences without counting the cost of their discipleship.

May the Holy Spirit guide us so that all our programmes, strategies, and theologies of mission will make us servants of the Kingdom of Jesus.

Selected Reflections by Thomas Merton

You do not need to know precisely what is happening, or exactly where it is all going. What you need is to recognize the possibilities and challenges offered by the present moment, and to embrace them with courage, faith and hope . . . Our job is to love others without stopping to enquire whether or not they are worthy. That is nobody's business. What we are asked to do is to love, and that love itself will render both ourselves and our neighbours worthy . . . Just remaining quietly in the presence of God, listening to Him, being attentive to Him, requires a lot of courage and know-how.[137]

Biographical notes on the Sisters

since leaving The Clarences

Sister Philippa Green, IBVM (Loreto)

Figure 18: Sister Philippa Green, IBVM (Loreto)

During the Loreto Sisters' ministry in The Clarences, Philippa's passion for education, her training in child guidance, and her work as an educational psychologist were invaluable assets. Recalling her previous employment in the Moss Side Child Guidance and School Psychological Service in Manchester, a former colleague said of her: "Philippa's wit and wisdom, together with her understanding of, and compassion for, the human condition, enhanced the team's practice beyond measure and contributed to its collective learning in ways that endure in these individuals, personally and professionally, to the present time."

After responding to her order's call for "a preferential option for the poor", and being "missioned" in 1988 for grass roots ministry, her move to the North East was challenging to say the least. Both Sisters felt they had been called to work in an entirely new direction, but they embarked on this pioneering venture without any certainty of what their mission might be or of what they might be called to do. Philippa's previous experience stood her in good stead, both in enabling her to find work to augment their income and in providing much-needed pastoral care on the estate. Working as part of a close-knit team, she complemented Imelda's more active role in helping to bring about change. As Jean Orridge, the headteacher of High Clarence Primary School, remembered:

> Sister Philippa was passionate about supporting the families and this could be observed in the love and care she showed for them, especially the children. In Sister Philippa they found a true friend, who listened, advised, encouraged, and supported whatever issues they faced.

After leaving The Clarences, Philippa had a profound call to become a solitary, to spend the rest of her time searching for God. Her Superior General discerned this call with her and officially sent her to this mission. She initially spent a short time at Seahouses on the Northumberland coast before settling at Glen Conwy. For the first three years she was also Vice Provincial for the English Province, but she remained steadfast to her contemplative way of life to the end. However, after being diagnosed with cancer she moved back to the North East and lived for a year as a solitary in York. This gave her great joy as she courageously faced her impending death. She spent her last few weeks at the Loreto House in Llandudno, Wales. She died on New Year's Eve 2014, aged 77 and in the fifty-ninth year of her religious life. Imelda was with her during her last days and when she died peacefully just before midnight.

Philippa, besides remaining faithful to Mary Ward, was inspired by some significant holy people. These included Mechthild of Magdeburg, Hildegard of Bingen, Thomas Merton, Teresa of Avila, John of the Cross, and the simplicity of Francis and Clare of Assisi. She also revered the Northumbrian saints—Bede, Cuthbert, Aidan, and Hilda. All of them were worked into the Prayers of the Faithful at her Requiem Mass. In her obituary, it was said of her:

> Those of us who knew her well will remember her many kindnesses, her sympathy and her passion for justice. We will remember her love of literature and the Arts. Above all we will remember, with a smile on our face, her great sense of humour and sharp, quick wit. She was born on the Feast of the Transfiguration. She will surely be saying with conviction: "It is good for me to be here." May she enjoy the fullness of the beatific vision.

Sister Imelda Poole, IBVM (Loreto)

Figure 19: Sister Imelda Poole, IBVM (Loreto)

Since leaving The Clarences in 2004, Imelda has been working in the field of anti-trafficking in Albania. She is a member of the English Province of the Institute of the Blessed Virgin Mary (IBVM). This has been done through the foundation RENATE (Religious in Europe Networking Against Trafficking and Exploitation), of which she is co-founder and President. Since 2013 her work in Albania has been supported by the Mary Ward Loreto Foundation (MWL), an NGO that aims to combat modern-day slavery. This challenging mission is implemented through works of justice, education, grassroots action, and systemic change. The call is to eradicate poverty, the prime cause of human trafficking. This vision is based on the philosophy and charism of Mary Ward, which inspires people to reach their full potential. Imelda is President of MWL.

In the field of prevention, projects have been established including the Mary Ward Loreto Women's Project, which works in 18 rural and informal areas of Albania. The goal is the human and economic empowerment of 3,000 women and it includes sixteen small local businesses. The Mary Ward Loreto Youth and Men's Projects work with 1,000 youth and men in many vulnerable regions and they, too, focus on human and economic empowerment. MWL has opened an advice centre in Tirana, the capital city of Albania, serving up to sixty abused and exploited women in the city. An education project, which includes service learning, has begun and has conducted nationwide research on ethics in the education system in Albania.

Notes

1   *Evening Gazette* (a Teesside newspaper based in Middlesbrough), June/
    August 1986.
2   In North America the original Italian spelling of Loretto is used.
3   Fr Austin Smith, in a keynote address delivered at the fourth International
    Stauros Congress on Powerlessness, Duquesne University, USA, June 1985.
    See also his *Passion for the Inner City: A Personal View* (Sheed and Ward,
    1983) and *Journeying with God: Paradigms of Power and Powerlessness* (Sheed
    and Ward, 1990). Fr Smith died in 2011 aged 82.
4   Teesport is now the third largest port in the UK and amongst the ten biggest
    in Western Europe.
5   The Stockton and Darlington Railway linked Stockton-on-Tees with coalfields
    in the Shildon area via Darlington. It was extended to Middlesbrough in 1831.
    See <http://en.wikipedia.org/wiki/Stockton_and_Darlington_Railway>.
6   The Clarence Railway was owned by a Londoner, Christopher Tennant. The
    line was taken over by the Stockton and Hartlepool Railway, a subsidiary
    of the Hartlepool Docks and Railway Company, to allow quicker onward
    shipment from Hartlepool's new docks. This became part of the North Eastern
    Railway in 1865. See <https://en.wikipedia.org/wiki/Clarence_Railway>.
7   Some of the historical information has been retrieved from <http://
    en.wikipedia.org/wiki/Port_Clarence> and <http://en.wikipedia.org/wiki/
    Haverton_Hill>.
8   See <http://www.gracesguide.co.uk/Isaac_Lowthian_Bell>.
9   I am indebted to Ann Appleton, brought up in Port Clarence, for invaluable
    information during this early period drawn from her MA dissertation on
    Local History (CNAA) at Teesside Polytechnic, "A Colony of Workmen: The
    Socio-Economic Development of Port Clarence 1851–1881" (<http://www.
    freewebs.com/portclarence/18511881.htm> created by Marsha Mulloy).

10   BBC on the internet: "Domesday Reloaded—Port Clarence and Haverton",
     <http://www.bbc.co.uk/history/domesday/dblock/GB-448000-522000/
     page/2>.

11   Mary Whitaker (née Appleton), "Growing up in Port Clarence in the
     1950s and 60s", in Appleton, MA dissertation (<http://www.freewebs.com/
     portclarence/1950s1960s.htm> created by Marsha Mulloy).

12   Cited in Appleton, MA dissertation. Florence Bell's book was published by
     Ernest Arnold (London, 1907).

13   Louise Gwynne-Jones, "Seal Sands: 1000 years of Industry alongside Nature"
     (<http://www.stocktonteesside.co.uk/seal-sands---teesmouth-national-
     nature-reserve.html>). By the sixteenth century, this profitable salt industry
     had been eclipsed by that of South Shields. Boreholes were also sunk in
     Cowper Marsh.

14   It was first called the Government Nitrogen Factory. Brunner Mond renamed
     it the Synthetic Ammonia and Nitrates Company.

15   See <https://en.wikipedia.org/wiki/Billingham_Manufacturing_Plant>. New
     industries included plastics for aircraft cockpits, and synthetic petrol made
     from hydrogenated carbon (coal) for aircraft fuel. In the Second World War,
     atomic research also took place on the site and a nuclear reactor was later
     developed there.

16   Retrieved from <http://en.wikipedia.org/wiki/Haverton_Hill> and "Furness
     Shipbuilding Co" from *Grace's Guide to British Industrial History* (<http://
     gracesguide.co.uk/Furness_Shipbuilding_Co>). The yard was part of the
     Furness, Withy and Co shipbuilding empire based at Hartlepool and built
     colliers, tramps, deep-sea tankers, diesel-electric ships (the first in the North
     Sea), whaling vessels, and twin-funnelled passenger/cargo liners.

17   See <http://en.wikipedia.org/wiki/Tees_Transporter_Bridge>. It is one of
     only three in Britain.

18   The BBC programme was in the third series of *Auf Wiedersehen, Pet* (2002).

19   Whitaker, "Growing up in Port Clarence".

20   The 2011 Census gave the High Clarence population as 773.

21   Farrar, Straus and Cudahy, 1958.

22   Catherine Cookson received an OBE in 1985 and was created a Dame of the
     British Empire in 1993. On her death, she left most of her fortune to charity.

23   Ellen Wilkinson, *The Town That Was Murdered* (Victor Gollancz, 1939).

[24] Geoff Miller, "The Feast of St Cuthbert, Bishop of Lindisfarne", St Nicholas' Cathedral, Newcastle-upon-Tyne, November 2000.

[25] Thomas Ward, *Gazette Live*, <http://www.gazettelive.co.uk/>, April 2012.

[26] Information in the following sections is drawn from a number of reports, including the social entrepreneur research reports and articles, and from the IBVM Sisters' reports and personal interviews. See also Jeanne Hinton, "Laying Ghosts in Teesside" in Hinton, *Changing Churches: Building Bridges in Local Mission* (Churches Together in Britain and Ireland, 2002), pp. 72–79.

[27] Ofsted report for High Clarence Primary School, October 2013, <https://reports.ofsted.gov.uk/provider/files/2278533/urn/111523.pdf>.

[28] Lucy Richardson, *The Northern Echo*, 5 December 2013.

[29] <http://www.bbc.co.uk/news/uk-england-tees-17431427>.

[30] *Evening Gazette*, June/August 1986.

[31] Cited in "Toxic Waste", *The Economist*, October 2000, p. 41.

[32] The main employers at this time were the Bell Brothers, Clarence Iron Works, The Salt Union Ltd, United Alkali Company Ltd, Anderston Foundry Company, the Cement Works at Haverton Hill, and The Coal Distribution Company at Port Clarence.

[33] Margaret Hebblethwaite (ed.), *The Living Spirit: Prayers and Readings for the Christian Year* (Rowman and Littlefield, 2000), p. 194.

[34] *A Manual of Anglo-Catholic Devotion* (Hymns Ancient and Modern, 2000), p. 7.

[35] The Venerable Bede, ed. Judith McClure and Roger Collins, *The Ecclesiastical History of the English People*, (Oxford University Press, 1999), p. 227. See also <http://www.hermitary.com/articles/cuthbert.html>.

[36] Information on Mary Ward and the Loreto Sisters has been drawn from material sent to me by Imelda Poole, IBVM (Loreto), or retrieved from the internet: <https://en.wikipedia.org/wiki/Mary_Ward_(nun)>; <http://en.wikipedia.org/wiki/Sisters_of_Loreto>; <http://www.bar-convent.org.uk/maryward.htm>.

[37] Henriette Peters, tr. Helen Butterworth, *Mary Ward: A World in Contemplation* (Gracewing, 1994).

[38] Mary Ward, 1609, quoted in Peters, *Mary Ward*, p. 95.

[39] Pope Pius V (1566–1572) had ruled that solemn vows and strict papal enclosure were essential to all communities of religious women. Their work

was confined to teaching boarding students within the cloister or nursing the sick in hospitals attached to the monastery.

40 Mary Ward, 1617.

41 See <http://www.bar-convent.org.uk/maryward.htm>

42 Selected writings of Mary Ward in modern English can be found in Gillian Orchard IBVM (ed.), *Till God Will: Mary Ward through her Writings* (Darton, Longman and Todd, 1985).

43 <http://www.stbedes.org.uk/mar-ward-the-mary-association>.

44 See <https://en.wikipedia.org/wiki/Mary_Ward_(nun)>.

45 See "Establishment of the Institute" (online, see note 37). See also Gemma Simmonds CJ, "Mary Ward: Then and now" at <https://www.thinkingfaith. org/articles/20100122_1.htm>, posted 22 January 2010.

46 In North America the original spelling of Loretto is used.

47 Mother Teresa was part of the Congregation from 1928 until 1950, during which time she founded the Missionaries of Charity in Calcutta.

48 IBVM Direction Statement.

49 See the IBVM's Mission Statement (Chapter 6, page 52).

50 Quoted at <https://www.congregationofjesus.org.uk/spirituality/ mary-ward-2/>.

51 Imelda Poole, "Grassroots Ministry: A Mary Ward Mission in the Twentieth Century", unpublished report, c. late 1990s.

52 Ibid.

53 Ibid. See also David J. Bosch, *Transforming Mission: Paradigm Shifts in Theology of Mission* (Orbis Books, 1991), pp. 390–92, 519.

54 Much of this section is based on Imelda Poole, "Transforming Mission", unpublished MS, c. late 1990s. She drew some of her ideas from Oliver Davies, *A Theology of Compassion: Metaphysics of Difference and the Renewal of Tradition* (SCM Press, 2001).

55 Hinton, *Changing Churches*, p. 72.

56 Imelda Poole's unpublished MS, "Spirituality in The Clarences", c. late 1990s.

57 Quoted in Hinton, *Changing Churches*, p. 75. The NESF was established in 1993 to advise government on how to combat long-term unemployment, and from 1997 on how to achieve greater inclusion in government plans: not that these moves necessarily had much effect in communities like The Clarences.

58 *Silence* (a book of poetry by Samuel Miller Hageman, 1848-1905; republished by Forgotten Books, 2012).

59 For further information see Janet Hodgson, *The Faith We See: Working with Images of Christ* (Inspire/Methodist Publishing House, 2006); *Making the Sign of the Cross: A Creative Resource for Seasonal Worship, Retreats and Quiet Days* (Canterbury Press, 2010); *Seeing Our Faith: Creative Ideas for Working with Images of Christ* (Canterbury Press, 2011).

60 The poem, written by Minnie Louise Haskins, was published in London in 1908 as part of a collection called *The Desert*. It is a particular favourite of Queen Elizabeth, who has used it on family memorials.

61 This poem is by Henry Scott Holland (1847–1918), Regius Professor of Divinity at Oxford University. It was based on a sermon he gave in St Paul's Cathedral in May 1910 following the death of King Edward VII.

62 The knitting yarn is threaded onto tapestry needles. The stitching of the cross and the edges, which bind the sachet, is embroidered diagonally.

63 For further information on holding crosses, see Hodgson, *Making the Sign of the Cross*, pp. 108–9.

64 Vera Mae Thomas seems to have come from Huntington, Texas.

65 This section is largely drawn from Hodgson, *The Faith We See*, pp. 27–30.

66 Imelda Poole to Janet Hodgson, 23 March 2015.

67 Written specially for this book.

68 Much of this material is drawn from Hodgson, *The Faith We See*, Chapter 3.

69 Laurie Green, *Let's Do Theology: A Pastoral Cycle Resource Book* (Mowbray, 1990), p. 4.

70 See Hodgson, *The Faith We See*, pp. 27–9.

71 Albert Nolan, Institute of Contextual Theology, n.d., p. 3.

72 Ibid.

73 John Pridmore, "Diary", *Church Times,* 18 February 2000.

74 Nolan, quoted in Larry Kaufmann, "Good News to the Poor: The Impact of Albert Nolan in South Africa", in McGlory T. Speckman and Larry T. Kaufmann (eds), *Towards an Agenda for Contextual Theology: Essays in Honour of Albert Nolan* (Cluster Publications, 2001), p. 7. See also Nolan, ICT, n.d., pp. 1–3; Hodgson, *The Faith We See*, pp. 27–30.

75 Desmond Tutu, *God Has a Dream: A Vision of Hope for Our Time* (Rider, 2004), p. 109.

76 The order's Vision Statement is as follows: "We are called to promote the Glory of God, following the person of Jesus, lovingly discerning God's will by endeavouring to fulfil Mary Ward's vision where the values of love, freedom,

sincerity and justice are experienced and lived out by all." (See, for example, <http://www.loreto.in/vision.aspx>).

[77] Recently, Tim Lomax has argued that a contextual approach should be used in devising creative Anglican missional worship by drawing on today's language and cultural forms. The liturgy would then be both sacramental and incarnational: *Creating Missional Worship: Fusing Context and Tradition* (Church House Publishing, 2015).

[78] The Teesside National Nature Reserve is now designated a Site of Special Scientific Interest and an international site of importance for waterbirds.

[79] The Society of St Vincent de Paul is an international Catholic voluntary organization dedicated to the sanctification of its members through caring for the poor and disadvantaged.

[80] Personal communication, 27 November 2007.

[81] Interview with Jon Sobrino by Joe Drexler-Dreis, *Newsletter CLT* 6, September 2013 (<https://theo.kuleuven.be/en/research/centres/centr_lib/interview-with-jon-sobrino.pdf>).

[82] Jon Sobrino, tr. Robert R. Barr, *Spirituality of Liberation: Toward Political Holiness* (Orbis Books, 1988). His other books include *Jesus the Liberator: A Historical-Theological Reading of Jesus of Nazareth* (Continuum 1994), *Christ the Liberator: A View from the Victims* (Orbis 2001), *Christology at the Crossroads: A Latin American Approach* (Wipf & Stock, 2002), *The True Church and the Poor* (Orbis, 1985), *The Principle of Mercy: Taking the Crucified People from the Cross* (Orbis, 1994), *No Salvation Outside the Poor: Prophetic-Utopian Essays* (Orbis, 2008).

[83] The wording of both quotations, translated from the original Spanish, varies slightly in different sources.

[84] Cited in Michael Mott, *The Seven Mountains of Thomas Merton* (Houghton Mifflin, 1984), p. 550. See also Thomas Merton, *The Seven Storey Mountain: An Autobiography of Faith* (Harcourt Brace, 1948).

[85] The Anglican Communion has five Marks of Mission but they embrace much "doing", starting with "Proclaiming the Good News". Listening is not one of the marks: Janet Hodgson, *Good News Story Workshops: Based on the Five Marks of Mission* (Grove Books, EV 95, 2011).

[86] Published by SCM Press, 2015.

[87]   CAP was formed in 1982 with its headquarters in Manchester. For further information, see <http://en.wikipedia.org/wiki/Church_Action_on_Poverty> and CAP's own website at <http://www.church-poverty.org.uk/>.

[88]   Quotations from "Poverty Unmasked: Teesside Poverty Hearing", Teesside Church Action on Poverty, May 1995.

[89]   E.g. Rupert Hambira, *See, Judge, Act—Five Bible Studies for Transformation* (The Congregational Federation, 1996); *Challenge to the Church: A Theological Comment on the Political Crisis in South Africa (The Kairos Document)*, (The Kairos Theologians, 1985); *Evangelical Witness in South Africa: A Critique of Evangelical Theology and Practice by South African Evangelicals* (Concerned Evangelicals, Eerdmans, 1986); *A Relevant Pentecostal Witness* (anti-apartheid paper published by a Pentecostal group in 1988); and *The Road To Damascus: Kairos and Conversion* (Institute of Contextual Theology and Skotaville Publishers, 1989).

[90]   Nolan, *Contextual Theology,* p. 17.

[91]   Ibid., pp. 18–20. See also Green, *Let's Do Theology.*

[92]   Information for this case study was drawn from CAP newsletters and reports by David Cross, and Janet's own involvement in the Teesside CAP group during 2000 and 2001.

[93]   See also Hinton, *Changing Churches*, pp. 75–76.

[94]   E.g. Hinton, *Changing Churches*, pp. 72–79.

[95]   See <http://www.freshexpressions.org.uk> and <http://community.sharethe guide.org/ask/define>. The definition is a compilation of information given on the internet.

[96]   Ibid. For related internet sites and statistical information compiled by the Church Army Research Unit, see <http://www.freshexpressions.org.uk/research>.

[97]   Pioneer Ministry in the Church of England: see <https://www.cofepioneer.org>, and <http://freshexpressions.org.uk/get-started/pioneer-ministry/>. See also Cathy Ross and Jonny Baker (eds), *Pioneering Spirituality: Resources for Reflection and Practice* (Canterbury Press, 2015).

[98]   This selection of books on the subject is placed in historical order of publication: *Encounters on the Edge*, a critical analysis of case studies of new fresh expressions of church, mostly still in the making, published by the Church Army Resource Unit, Sheffield, 1999–2013 (which I received monthly); Sally Gaze, *Mission-shaped and Rural: Growing Churches in the*

Countryside, (Church House Publishing (CHP), 2006); Steven Croft (ed.), *Mission-shaped Questions: Defining Issues for Today's Church* (CHP, 2008); Martin Percy and Louise Nelstrop (eds), *Evaluating Fresh Expressions: Explorations in Emerging Church* (Canterbury Press, 2008); The Mission-shaped Church Working Group, chaired by Graham Cray, *Mission-shaped Church: Church Planting and Fresh Expressions of Church in a Changing Context* (2nd edn, CHP, 2009); David Goodhew, Andrew Roberts, Michael Volland, *Fresh! An Introduction to Fresh Expressions of Church and Pioneer Ministry* (SCM Press, 2012).

99 Steven Croft, Ian Mobsby (eds), *Ancient Faith, Future Mission: Fresh Expressions in the Sacramental Tradition* (Canterbury Press, 2009). Contributors include Rowan Williams, Steve Croft, Stephen Cottrell, Ian Mobsby, Richard Giles, Phyllis Tickle, Karen Ward, and Brian McLaren.

100 Bob Jackson, *The Road to Growth: Towards a Thriving Church* (2015), *Going for Growth: What Works at Local Church Level* (2006), and *What Makes Churches Grow? Vision and Practice in Effective Mission* (2015) (all Church House Publishing).

101 David Goodhew (ed.), *Towards a Theology of Church Growth* (Ashgate, 2015). See also the report and video: Church Growth Research Programme: fresh expressions in the Church of England (<http://community.sharetheguide.org/sites/default/files/churchgrowthresearch-freshexpressions.pdf> and <https://vimeo.com/84310265>).

102 Fr Jay Kothare to Janet Hodgson, 28 December 2015.

103 This area was notorious as a site where children were burnt as offerings to the god Moloch. Jeremiah described it as a hell on earth where "the blood of the innocent was spilled" (cf. Jeremiah 7. 30-32 and Jeremiah 19. 1-6).

104 *Gazette Live,* 14 June 2013.

105 Information taken from Gazette Live, *Evening Gazette*, Mail Online, *The Northern Echo*, 2011–2015, on the internet.

106 See <https://www.ilivehere.co.uk/statistics-port-clarence-middlesbrough-30991.html>.

107 The data was provided by the Office of National Statistics.

108 Church Action on Poverty North East Annual Report, September 2011–January 2013. CAP North East was launched in 1988 following on from the Dominican conference on "The Churches' Option for the Poor" (<http://

www.church-poverty.org.uk/groups/north-east/annualreview/2013/annual report2013>).

[109] The Billingham Legacy Foundation was founded in 2010 with residents creating an endowment trust fund for the benefit of the wider Billingham community. The interest from this Legacy Fund is used for charitable giving to those most in need in local groups and associations. Government cuts in funding have meant that, in 2014 alone, 28 grants amounting to £12,000 were dispensed in response to requests.

[110] This was part of the HLF Tees Transporter Bridge Visitor Experience Project.

[111] See the Augean website (<http://www.augeanplc.com/>) and click on Waste Management and Landfill for details on hazardous or non-hazardous waste, with contact details. The treatment process of hazardous material is given in detail.

[112] Biomass Energy had plans for a power station on these brownfield sites too, which would have created many jobs, but these plans collapsed. The proposal was to erect a reversible energy factory to turn waste into energy. The non-reversible waste from recyclable waste would have been dumped in landfill sites.

[113] Neil Macfarlane, *Evening Gazette*, Middlesbrough, 13 September 2015: <https://www.questia.com/newspaper/1G1-250580821/nuclear-bomb-waste-dumped-in-teesside-exclusive>.

[114] Ibid.

[115] Ibid. The Augean site also operates a chemical treatment centre, which is able to treat a wide range of acidic and alkaline liquid waste by processing with air pollution control residues. The fully automated system is considered to be state-of-the-art in the waste industry.

[116] Matthew Fox (ed.), *Illuminations of Hildegard of Bingen* (Bear and Company, 1985), p. 8.

[117] Tristar Homes report on Port Clarence, 2014: <http://www.tristarhomes.co.uk/rte.asp?id=332> (Tristar Homes is now part of Thirteen Housing Group, and this report is no longer accessible).

[118] Ibid.

[119] The story of this first Christmas party was sent to me by Pat Chambers, 12 November 2015.

[120] *Billingham Community Newspaper*, September 2015, p. 24.

121 CRAG has also joined forces with HEAL, a Stockton organization concerned with Health, Exercise and Allotments, funded by Catalyst.

122 The *BCN* is an independent newspaper funded by sponsorship and advertisements. Seventeen local sponsors are listed in the September 2015 issue, ranging from local shops, accountants, and colleges to an environmental trust. The tabloid now numbers 32 pages. Each issue costs £3,000 to produce and only reports good news about good people achieving great things. The newspaper aims to showcase groups and associations, signpost community connections, raise aspirations, and inspire a community to know and help their neighbours. Available online at <http://www.billinghamcommunity newspaper.co.uk/>.

123 The quotation is from "The Lorax" by Theodor Seuss Geisel, *Dr Seuss* (Random House, 1971). In November 2015, *BCN* was the outright winner of the Community Minded Business Award as part of the Cleveland Police Safety Awards for the whole Tees Valley, stretching from Redcar to Stockton and Hartlepool. Pat Chambers, the editor, was finalist in the *Evening Gazette* Trinity Group Community Champions Awards: Pat Chambers to Janet Hodgson, 26 November 2015. See also <http://www.billinghamcommunity newspaper.co.uk/a-community-minded-business/>.

124 The Billingham Team Ministry now includes churches in the outlying communities of Port Clarence, Newton Bewley, Cowpen Bewley, and large industrial areas on the eastern outskirts of Billingham, stretching to the banks of the River Tees and the former salt flats.

125 From the "Spiritual Maxims" of Brother Lawrence.

126 From her song "O viriditas".

127 BELP's address is Hereford Terrace, Cowpen Training Centre, Billingham, TS23 4AA. Telephone: 01642 564077. For more information see <http://www. teesvalleyfoundation.org/donors/belp> and <http://www.mrmarchitectural services.com/belp.html>.

128 Using MRM 3D modelling and digital terrain in software, they are able to produce accurate architectural images needed for such projects. See BELP's promotional material.

129 Mike Blackburn, <http://www.gazettelive.co.uk/news/local-news/ex-police-chief-up-community-champions-3678919>, May 2013, and see also Lyndsay Oxley, <http://www.gazettelive.co.uk/news/teesside-news/community-champions-2014-winners-stories-8230946>, December 2014.

[130] <http://www.billinghamcommunitynewspaper.co.uk/kevin-pitt-wins-catalyst-outstanding-achievement-award/>. Catalyst are financial markets experts. Their work includes developing leadership and change (<http://www.catalyst.co.uk>). Kevin is also a founder and Vice-Chairman of the Billingham Legacy Foundation and was recently elected to the Northern Locality Forum.

[131] The site is part of a £300,000 package for the area. According to Groundwork's mission statement: "Together we can improve properties and create green places. Act now!" (<http://www.groundwork.org.uk/>).

[132] The management team includes Deryck Forrest as Horticulture Director and Jennifer Franklin as Administration Director, together with a site supervisor and a supervisor for project training and programmes.

[133] Groundwork has recently built an impressive triple jump track in the garden.

[134] "NCS in Port Clarence", *BCN*, September/October 2015.

[135] See *BCN*, September/October 2015; <http://www.billinghamcommunity newspaper.co.uk/ncs-in-port-clarence/>.

[136] *BCN*, September/October 2015, and "Port Clarence volunteers for makeover", September 2015, <http://www.augeanplc.com/pcallotment/default. aspx>. The Thirteen Housing Group has created a separate Beech Terrace Community Garden for local residents, including a children's play area. The official opening took place in December 2015. A local choir sang carols and Jean Orridge switched on the Christmas lights. The residents then took part in a wreath-laying ceremony at the war memorial, followed by the annual Christmas party. See <http://www.billinghamcommunitynewspaper.co.uk/festive-opening-for-new-community-garden/>, January 2016.

[137] Based on the reflections of Thomas Merton; sources include Contemplation in a World of Action (1971).

Lightning Source UK Ltd.
Milton Keynes UK
UKHW02f0941150118
316165UK00011B/596/P